THE SACRAMENTAL MAGIC OF ADVENT

THE SACRAMENTAL MAGIC OF ADVENT
A Guide to Christian Ceremonial Ritual at Christmas

by
Stephen Mandes Thomas

AEON

First published in 2025 by
Aeon Books

Copyright © 2025 by Stephen Mandes Thomas

The right of Stephen Mandes Thomas to be identified as the author of this work has been asserted in accordance with §§ 77 and 78 of the Copyright Design and Patents Act 1988.

All rights reserved. No part of this publication may be reproduced, stored in a retrieval system, or transmitted, in any form or by any means, electronic, mechanical, photocopying, recording, or otherwise, without the prior written permission of the publisher.

British Library Cataloguing in Publication Data

A C.I.P. for this book is available from the British Library

ISBN-13: 978-1-80152-195-6

Typeset by Medlar Publishing Solutions Pvt Ltd, India

www.aeonbooks.co.uk

CONTENTS

INTRODUCTORY MATERIAL

INTRODUCTION   xiii

ABOUT THIS BOOK   xxi

A GUIDE TO MAGICAL PHILOSOPHY   xxv

I. ADVENT

PART ONE: PREPARATION

Getting started   5

CHAPTER ONE
The history and purpose of advent   7

CHAPTER TWO
How to fast   11

CHAPTER THREE
Prayer and meditation — 15

CHAPTER FOUR
Charity — 19

PART TWO: FIRST WEEK OF ADVENT

CHAPTER FIVE
First Sunday in Advent — 27

CHAPTER SIX
The Advent Wreath — 29

CHAPTER SEVEN
Advent and the Second Coming — 31

CHAPTER EIGHT
The Guardian Angel — 39

CHAPTER NINE
Saint Andrew's Day — 43

CHAPTER TEN
The Christmas Tree — 49

CHAPTER ELEVEN
Foundations of Christian Magic: The Sign of the Cross — 55

PART THREE: SECOND WEEK OF ADVENT

CHAPTER TWELVE
Second Sunday in Advent — 63

CHAPTER THIRTEEN
Saint Nicholas Day — 67

CHAPTER FOURTEEN
The Immaculate Conception — 75

CHAPTER FIFTEEN
Foundations of Christian Magic: Almsgiving and Offerings — 81

PART FOUR: THIRD WEEK OF ADVENT

CHAPTER SIXTEEN
Third Sunday in Advent (Guadete Sunday) — 89

CHAPTER SEVENTEEN
Saint Lucy's Day — 93

CHAPTER EIGHTEEN
Ember Days — 97

CHAPTER NINETEEN
Foundations of Christian Magic: Forgiveness — 103

PART FIVE: FOURTH WEEK OF ADVENT

CHAPTER TWENTY
Fourth Sunday in Advent — 109

CHAPTER TWENTY ONE
Saint Thomas's Day — 113

CHAPTER TWENTY TWO
The Winter of Solstice — 119

CHAPTER TWENTY THREE
Foundations of Christian Magic: Consecrating sacramentals — 123

II. CHRISTMAS

CHAPTER TWENTY FOUR
Christmas Eve — 133

CHAPTER TWENTY FIVE
Christmas Day — 137

CHAPTER TWENTY SIX
Saint Stephen's Day — 149

CHAPTER TWENTY SEVEN
Saint John's Day — 153

CHAPTER TWENTY EIGHT
The Feast of the Holy Innocents — 157

CHAPTER TWENTY NINE
Saint Thomas Becket — 161

CHAPTER THIRTY
The Holy Family — 165

CHAPTER THIRTY ONE
New Year's Eve and New Year's Day — 169

CHAPTER THIRTY TWO
Eve of Epiphany — 173

CHAPTER THIRTY THREE
Epiphany — 175

CHAPTER THIRTY FOUR
The Epiphany initiation — 179

AFTERWORD: *The Christian wheel of the year* — 183

APPENDICES

APPENDIX A
A list of commonly used prayers — 187

APPENDIX B
Making your own holy water — 199

APPENDIX C
Psalms and their magical uses — 203

APPENDIX D
A brief guide to incense — 207

APPENDIX E
Correspondences of the tradition planets and the four elements — 213

APPENDIX F
Additional resources — 215

APPENDIX G
Calendars for Agent and Christmas for 2025–2035 — 217

APPENDIX H
Notes — 221

ACKNOWLEDGEMENTS — 223

INDEX — 225

INTRODUCTORY MATERIAL

INTRODUCTION

Welcome, Seeker!

This book is a complete course of initiation into Christian magic, mysticism, and tradition, focusing on the season of Advent and the Christmas celebration which follows it. It is the second book in the Sacramental Magic series, following *The Book of Sacramental Magic*.

The previous book in this series presented an in-depth system of Christian magic and ritual. This book is the first of several which will focus on the Christian liturgical cycle, or what we might call the "Christian Wheel of the Year."

Traditional Christianity is organized around ritual practices, the sacramentals and sacraments, including the rosary, the many customs surrounding the saints, and, of course, the mass. It is also organized around *time*. The previous book in this series focused on the first of these concepts; this book focuses on the second. Just as traditional religion sees physical space as a spiritual landscape, marked by sacred places like churches and shrines, so too it sees the progression of time as a spiritual cycle, marked by sacred days and seasons, fasts and feasts. As magical practitioners, we are able to make use of these sacred seasons in our practice. As ordinary religious believers, we are called to participate in them, as they form a key part of the foundation of the

Church as a whole. Like every book in this series, *The Sacramental Magic of Advent* approaches the matter from both sides at once: that is, for magical practitioners who hope to incorporate traditional Christian religion into their practice, and ordinary believers who hope to re-incorporate traditional Christian magic into their faith.

If you're coming to this book after having read and worked through *The Book of Sacramental Magic*, you should know that there are some important differences between that book and this one. *The Book of Sacramental Magic* focuses on ritual and magical philosophy, and is primarily intended for the solo practitioner. This book includes rituals, including many which will be new to you, but the focus is on tradition, and much of it is suitable for work in a group or family setting. The magical philosophy presented will already be familiar to you. *The Book of Sacramental Magic* may be taken up and worked with at any time of the year. This book, on the other hand, is primarily relevant to the seasons of Advent and Christmas. The two books are not mutually exclusive: You can read and work with this before The Book of Sacramental Magic, as it provides a much gentler introduction to the magical system as a whole. You can work with it after The Book of Sacramental Magic, in order to expand and enhance your work with our tradition. And you can work with the two books at the same time. How you approach this is up to you.

If you are new to the system of Sacramental Magic, or to the concepts of magic or specifically of Christian magic, it may help to define a few of our terms before we proceed.

Initiation

We can define an "initiation" as any kind of structured course of study and practice, usually culminating in a final ritual, whose final result produces an enduring change in the life and the soul of the initiate. You will notice that that definition is broad enough to encompass a great many things—the sacraments of Baptism and Confirmation, the degrees of a fraternal order like the Freemasons or the Knights of Columbus, or the related degrees of a magical order like the Society of the Inner Light are initiations. But so is the completion of a boot camp, the earning of a black belt in a martial art, and even getting a driver's license!

In the course of study outlined in this book, we're interested in three things. The first is the traditional Christian approach to the seasons of Advent and Christmas through fasting, prayer, spiritual reading, and meditation. The second is the whole panoply of interesting, fun, and often very strange customs of celebrating the many festivals of this season that have come down to us through the centuries from our forebears in Christian Europe. The third is a simple but complete and effective system of magic.

Magic

Of course, the next thing to do is to define that tricky word, "magic."
Here are three competing definitions:

1. Attempting to influence the course of events with the aid of the Devil or other evil spirits, or any spirit other than God.
2. The art and science of causing changes in consciousness in accordance with the will.
3. Anything wonderful and exciting in a way that suggests the operation of more-than-ordinary forces.

The first definition is that used by the Catholic Church. We will come back to it in a moment.

The third definition is by far the most common in ordinary use. Have you ever heard someone talk about the "magic of Hollywood," or describe a good time by saying, "It was a truly magical evening"? Or have you ever heard the songs "This Magic Moment" by the Drifters or "Do You Believe in Magic?" by The Lovin' Spoonful? This is what they were talking about. I know you're smart enough to understand that someone who told you they had a magical time on their vacation didn't mean they spent the week summoning demons! But they are talking about something real and important, and something which is very much a part of this book.

The trouble comes in with that second definition, "The art and science of causing changes in consciousness in accordance with will." This is the definition of magic given by the 20th-century occultist Dion Fortune. According to Fortune's definition, an act of magic could be magical in the third sense of being strange and wonderful, but also magical in the first sense of invoking the aid of evil spirits. If that's the case, it's forbidden to Christians.

On the other hand, an act which meets the second definition could be magical in its own sense and in the third sense. That is, it could cause a definite change in consciousness and also be wonderful and exciting in a way that suggests the operation of more-than-ordinary forces—and be perfectly Christian. In fact, by this definition the Mass itself is one of the great works of magic of all time.

So let's be very clear: By the first definition of magic given above, that held by the Roman Catholic Church at its most orthodox, this book will include no magic whatsoever.

By the definition of Dion Fortune, this is a book of magic. It is structured as a course of study, designed to instruct the student in the practice of magic and initiate them into a current of magical power. Please note: The second part of the definition, "changes in consciousness in accordance with will." This is where it is very important to discuss precisely whose will we are talking about. In certain corners of the occult community, a concept of "finding one's true will" is considered to be very important indeed. In practice, however, the "true will" almost always turns out to be "whatever you want at any given moment." And so we need to be clear that the true will for the believing Christian means nothing more or less than the Will of God for you in this lifetime and the life to come.

By the common definition, I very much hope that this will be a magical book. As pithy and commonplace as the common definition sounds, in a way it is the most important. It is the feeling of many that our world has become sterile, stale and disenchanted. Even our (very few) holidays are pale shadows of what they once were. It is the goal of this book to re-enchant the Christmas season through the rediscovery of our ancient customs and traditions, and thus to bring a new spiritual light to a world grown tired of bland materialism.

Tradition

The traditions discussed in this book are the festival customs of European Christendom and its descendants, especially in the United States of America. I do not discuss customs from elsewhere in the world. There are two major reasons for that. The first is simply that these are the traditions that I know, and to expand the scope of my research to the entire world would require me to devote several more years of writing to a book that would end up five times as long!

The second reason is that I'm writing in an American context, and in that context Catholics and other Christians from European ethnic backgrounds have very often lost contact with their own traditions, while non-European Catholics more frequently have not. Readers of any background may find the discussion of seasonal customs interesting, and are certainly invited to incorporate them into their lives and the lives of their families. The magical practices, meanwhile, are universal and may be of interest to readers of any background. But European-Americans—and particularly, at least in my experience, those of the German/Irish stock that forms the oldest core of American Catholicism—are far more likely to find them *necessary*. It is an unfortunate fact that those Catholic ethnic groups that have been established the longest in this country have lost more of their heritage than anyone else. And it would be one thing if the old customs were lost, only to be replaced with new American customs. Instead, they have largely been lost and replaced with nothing. It is my goal to remedy that.

And so I invite you, reader, to learn about the traditional customs of the old world of Christendom, incorporating what seems right to you and your family, leaving aside that which doesn't serve your needs.

The plan of this book

This book is divided into two main sections, Advent and Christmas, with a series of Appendixes at the end.

Part I: Advent is a guide through the four Sundays of Advent. During this time, we will pray and fast according to the old customs. We will encounter the traditions of Advent, from decorations to special foods to the feasts of important saints like Lucy, Nicholas, and Thomas. And we will work through a system of initiation into the magical side of the Christian tradition, which will finally culminate on Epiphany.

Part I is divided into four sections, each of which covers one of the four weeks of Advent. Under each week, you will find chapters of three different types. The first type consists of a reflection on the Sunday and the week in question, as well as Scripture readings and guides to prayer and meditation for that week. The second type consists of saints' days and other seasonal celebrations. These chapters include discussions of the saints, their history and legends, as well as traditional celebrations and guides to adapting those celebrations to the needs of the typical American home. The third type consists of more focused discussions of specific magical practices. These are always marked by the title "Foundations of Christian Magic." It's likely that one of these three will appeal to you more than the others. Esoteric Christians, Rosicrucians, and the like may be more interested in the sections on Christian magic, while more mainstream or traditional believers may prefer to skip those sections. This book is written for both of these types of people and everyone in between. You're welcome to use what works for you and leave the rest.

Part II: Christmas covers the celebrations of the Christmas season. Not just Christmas itself, but the whole 12-day cycle—and beyond. As mentioned above, this section culminates with a ritual of self-initiation on Epiphany, which makes use of the symbolism of the three magi presenting their gifts to the Christ Child to symbolize the whole work of Christian magic.

The practices given in this book build on themselves one piece at a time. The whole system begins with the First Day of Advent, whenever that may fall in a given year, and proceeds through the weeks of Advent and into the Christmas season proper. But there are a number of celebrations and saints' days which fall in the early part of Advent. If you are encountering this book for the first time, some of the practices given for those days will be more advanced than the stage at which you are currently. That's okay—just ignore the parts you aren't familiar with for now. Next year, you can start the whole process over again, incorporating all of the practices. This book isn't meant to be a "one and done" sort of thing, worked with one year and abandoned for the next, but it is intended to present practices that you can live and grow with, year after year.

Finally, the **Appendixes** include a prayer book, listing a number of common prayers in English and in Latin; a guide to additional sacramentals beyond those covered in the main text; a guide to the traditional planets and elements and their correspondences, including archangels and divine names; a guide to the proper use of incense; suggestions for further reading; and a calendar with dates for Advent for the next ten years.

A note on terminology

Throughout this book, I will be using the terms "esoteric" and "esotericism" to describe the practice of Christian magic as a whole. This term is meant as broadly as possible, as the Esoteric tradition includes a wide range of ideas, beliefs, and practices. Some of these are explicitly orthodox teachings that have simply been neglected in recent years. Others come from much further afield, drawing on the alternative traditions of Rosicrucianism, Gnosticism, Hermeticism and Neoplatonism. Whenever I present any idea, I will always discuss its source. That way, I don't have to switch back and forth between different terms like "traditional," "esoteric," and even "occult." At the same time, readers who are not interested in stepping outside of the doctrines of their own churches are given warning in advance when I am about to do so.

I also regularly use the terms "magic" and "magical," "myth," and "mythical." Readers are reminded to keep in mind the definition of magic given in the introduction, as this is always the meaning that is intended. The meaning of "myth" is something we will discuss at length in due time.

I have avoided the term "occult" entirely, due to its association, however unfair, in too many people's minds with witchcraft and working with evil spirits.

ABOUT THIS BOOK

This is the bit where I start talking about myself and my background; I usually skip these sections of the book. If you're like me, you can go ahead and jump past this part. I won't be offended. But I do think that if you're going to read a book like this, you have a right to know something about the author—where I'm coming from, what my background is, and what my approach is.

And so here's a little story.

I was raised in the Roman Catholic Church, in an out-of-the-way town in western Pennsylvania. The town itself was very Catholic, and my family was very Catholic.

Like many people of my generation, my experience of the Church was decidedly mixed. On the one hand, I believed in God, and I loved the traditions of the Church—holy days and fasts, saints, and angels. I particularly loved the Virgin Mary, who came to me in a vision when I was very young. On the other hand … Well. If you remember the Novus Ordo Catholic Church in the 1990s, you already know what's coming next. Mass was always a chore. The church itself looked like an auditorium, with garish modern art and a big, friendly Jesus smiling down from His cross. The songs ranged from the boring to the embarrassing. Unlike many modern congregations, we at least had incense and holy water—but not much else. Above all, it always felt like there was something missing. It was as though the church itself was like a beautiful, ancient painting that had been painted over with some insipid shade of beige. Here and there, the new paint flaked and fell away, and hints of the old majesty shone through. But it wasn't enough.

Of course, you won't be surprised to learn that the Church hierarchy was covering up a massive abuse scandal, even as they warned us all that Hell was waiting right around the next corner (especially if we spent too much time looking at the girls.)

And so, as many do, I wandered. In nature religions and magical traditions like Wicca, I found a hint of something that was missing in the Church—a sense of wonder and enchantment, the idea that magic permeated our everyday lives, and a way of celebrating the cycles of nature and the seasons of the year. But I didn't have the discipline necessary to commit to any sort of magical practice, even Wicca, and eventually I left that too for a life of vagrancy, petty crime and radical politics.

After many years, my life had reached its nadir. I was in my late 20s, living in an apartment in a slum in Southern California, making around $30 a day by transcribing documents. In desperation, I went searching for some of the magic that I had lost. I came across a book entitled *Modern Magick* by an author named Donald Michael Kraig. I'm ashamed to admit that I pirated the book from the internet, not even having the meager funds to pay for my own book.

And, opening the book, I was immediately horrified to discover that the system of magic it presented did not work with Pagan gods, much less demons, but with the angels and the God of the Christians! It even invoked God under names derived from the Old Testament!

Desperation is a powerful motivator. I had nothing left in my life, and so I proceeded. And two things happened. The first is simply that the rituals worked. From the very beginning—literally, from the first day—I was transformed. Overnight, my sleep cycle normalized, and my cravings for alcohol and nicotine plummeted. I started exercising every day, got my body into physical shape, and eventually found a career where I could support myself. Now, many years later, the work of magic has transformed me from a drunk and a petty criminal (petty only because I never had the courage to commit very large crimes) to a family man with a home, a career, a wife and two children.

The second thing that happened was, if anything, even more surprising. Invoking God every day by means of the Golden Dawn ritual,

I began to experience Him again as I had in my childhood. I found that He wasn't the terrifying intergalactic Stalinist from whom I had fled in my teenage years, but a loving father, a great fountain of power and majesty, presiding over a living universe filled to bursting with His angels and saints.

Before long, I discovered that this living universe of spirits wasn't something confined to weirdos and occultists, but had been the living tradition of the Church throughout the long years of that age which called itself Christendom, but which we dismiss as the "Middle Ages." I discovered the magical, but thoroughly Christian, philosophies of people like Marsilio Ficino and Cornelius Agrippa. And in so doing, I discovered everything that the Catholic Church, and most of the modern churches, have lost. In short, I discovered that the Christian tradition is a tradition of magic.

Now, I want to be clear about something. I did not then return to the Catholic Church as such. I do attend Mass from time to time, but the alternatives are the lifeless and empty Novus Ordo, on the one hand, and a "traditional" Church which is more focused on sin and hellfire, on the other. Instead, I turned to what is called the Esoteric Christian tradition. This is the tradition which is rooted in the great Christian philosophers of the past, including people like Dionysius the Areopagite and Thomas Aquinas, but also more radical thinkers like John Scotus Eriugena and Marsilio Ficino. The Esoteric tradition focuses on spiritual experience, rather than dogma, and it allows us the use of our reason. We all know that our Presbyterian neighbor or our aunt who was saved from an opiate addiction by turning to Buddhism aren't going to Hell. The Esoteric tradition allows us to state this openly, while providing a philosophical framework for understanding just what is happening with those people and others.

As I've continued my exploration of magic and esotericism, I've explored many other traditions as well. The tradition of Druidry, from the Celtic lands of Britain, has been a major source of spiritual sustenance to me, as have the Taoist traditions of China. I won't be talking much about those things in this book, but you should know that they are part of my background.

And so that's me.

What about you?

Maybe you're someone like me. An esotericist, occultist, magician—whatever you call yourself—who loves the practice of magic but finds themselves drawn to, or drawn back to, the traditions of the Christian churches. Maybe you're an otherwise ordinary member of a mainstream Church—a Catholic, or perhaps an Anglican or a Lutheran—who feels that their Church has lost something, some sort of spiritual power that it once had. And maybe you're somewhere in the middle.

This book is written for you, whoever you are. I won't try to hide my own views, and I make no apology for them. However, I do entirely respect the right of my readers to make their own judgments and to adhere to the teachings of their churches. If I'm going to share something which might be outside of the teachings of Church orthodoxy, I will say so, and you are free to skip that part. Or to focus on it, if that's what you prefer. Again, what I believe is what I believe. But if you believe differently—well, there is always the possibility that I am wrong and you are right!

This book won't please everyone; that's impossible. But I hope that it will please many of those who read it.

A GUIDE TO MAGICAL PHILOSOPHY

You can use this book without learning any magical philosophy at all. If you prefer to stick to a more orthodox way of doing things, you may either ignore the more explicitly magical practices, or make use of them without diving into the theories behind how they work. But some of it will make more sense and work more effectively if you understand the theory behind the practice.

And so we're going to explore two key magical concepts, which we'll call magical laws. The first is the Law of the Planes, and the second is the Law of Correspondence.

The Law of the Planes

The Law of the Planes tells us that the whole of the universe created by God is organized into a series of different levels. At the very highest level are spiritual forces like angels; at the lowest level is matter. God Himself relates to the planes in three different ways. He occupies the highest plane. He is also, at the same time, present throughout all the planes. And before this, he is both above and outside of all the planes.

Now, this universe of ours is complicated. Not only is it more complicated than humans understand, it's probably more complicated than we ever could understand. Because of this, there are many different ways of modeling the planes of existence. All of these should be understood as models only. While they point to reality, they aren't the same thing as reality. Their primary value is in their *usefulness*.

Please note: While no mainstream Church that I'm aware of uses the specific term "planes of existence," the idea of a layered universe is very much part of the mainstream Christian tradition. It can be found in the writings of Thomas Aquinas as well as Dionysius the Areopagite, and also in other, more esoterically inclined thinkers like the Renaissance philosopher (and priest) Marsilio Ficino.

The model of the planes we will use in this course is very simple and is derived from Ficino.

- First Plane: The Plane of Unity, also called the Divine Plane. This is the special plane of God Himself, which we can know only through the various Names of God given in the holy Scriptures.
- Second Plane: The Intellectual Plane. This is the Plane of the patterns of meaning which shape the material world. It is especially the plane of angels and saints.
- Third Plane: The Astral Plane. This is the plane of consciousness. All ordinary thinking takes place on the Astral Plane. It is also the plane of spirits, whether good, evil, or neutral. Finally, it is the plane where the subtle forces that shape our world emerge, especially the forces of astrology.
- Fourth Plane: The Energetic Plane. This is the plane of the Life Force. Not well understood in modern Western thought, the life force is the vital power that gives life to every living being and binds the world of nature together. Everything in nature has a life energy. In other traditions, this energy is called qi, ki, prana, and so on.
- Fifth Plane: The Material Plane. This is the plane of ordinary matter that we experience.

The plane of unity or the divine plane

The first plane is the plane reserved for God Himself. Please remember that it isn't God as such: God comes before all of the planes, and he is also present to all of them. Both in the writings of Dionysius the Areopagite and the mystical tradition of the Kabbalah, the Plane of Unity is seen as the Plane of the *Names of God*. In his treatise, *On the Divine Names*, Dionysius discusses many of these names, including the Good, Life, Light, Beauty,

Truth, and Wisdom. Each of these is a Name of God, not separate Gods. In Dionysius's thought, each of these names represents a kind of activity of God. These activities are not really separate from one another—but to us they appear to be. It's as though "The Good" were at once one of God's names, and something that God is doing. But, in a way that it's very hard or impossible for the human mind to grasp, "The Good" isn't truly separate from God's other Names, such as Life, Wisdom, and so on. All spiritual power ultimately begins on the Plane of Unity, and descends through the planes of being as far as the last of things.

The Intellectual Plane

After the Plane of Unity, this is the hardest for us to understand. Part of the reason has to do with language. In common English, the "intellect" means the thinking mind, and "an intellectual" is someone who spends a lot of time thinking about things and trying to learn things. But that isn't what is meant here. Instead, the Intellectual Plane is the plane of archetypal forces and patterns of meaning that shape our material world. To know something on the Intellectual Plane is to know it immediately and entirely, without any separation between the knower and the object of knowledge.

There are two types of beings who inhabit the Intellectual Plane. The first are eternal spirits, and the second are exalted human beings. We know the first group as angels, and the second group as saints.

On angels

Angels are spiritual beings created by God in order to govern the world, and for other tasks as well. In the Christian tradition, the angels are divided into nine hierarchies, and these nine are organized into three groups of three. The angels at each level are given a different task. The following description of them is derived from Dionysius's work *The Celestial Hierarchy* and the writings of Dom Gueranger in *The Liturgical Year*:

- Seraphim – Exalted, fiery spirits with six wings.
- Cherubim – Powerful beings depicted with four faces: one of a man, one of a lion, one of an eagle, and one of an ox.
- Thrones – Beings depicted as wheels with many eyes, that pull the chariot of God.

It can be very difficult to understand the work of the three highest of the angelic hierarchies, as they are very far removed from the world of our experience.

It is said that the Thrones act, as their name suggests, as the very throne of God. Of course, God is not a material being, and so he doesn't have a physical chair to sit on. Instead, this idea suggests that the Thrones somehow mediate between God Himself and His Creation, in the same way that a physical throne provides both a place where a king may be approached and a symbol of the monarch's authority. The Cherubim, with their many eyes, possess knowledge of all things save that which is known to God alone. The Seraphim sing the praises of God and purify the thoughts of those who stand before His throne. Medieval theologians suggested that these represent three paths of ascent to God: The Thrones represent the way of Justice; the Cherubim, the way of wisdom; and the Seraphim, the way of charity.

- Dominations – These preside over the government of the entire universe.
- Virtues – These angels watch over the course of nature's laws, the preservation of species, and the movements of the Heavens.
- Powers – The powers hold evil spirits in check.
- Principalities – Govern the human race as a whole and all large social groups, such as nations, cultures, churches, and so on.
- Archangels – These govern smaller groups like families and command the next order, the angels.
- Angels – These include the guardian angels who are set over every individual human soul.

Please note: The term "archangel" has a second meaning as well. It can also refer to any angel, from any hierarchy, who is in command of a group of angels, or who is set over a particular force like a planet or one of the elements of nature.

On saints

The word "saint" is a title, meaning "holy person," and it can refer to anybody in Heaven. When we address the angels, we add the word "Saint" to their name in the same way that we refer to someone on Earth as "Mister" or "Doctor" or "General." But it especially refers to those human beings who have transcended life on Earth and now dwell in Heaven with God. In the terms we're using here, the saints are human beings who have developed, through the Grace of God and their own spiritual practice, the ability to live on the Intellectual Plane and are now able to shape the world of human affairs, in accordance with the Will of God.

Now, there is some disagreement between the mainstream churches and the esoteric tradition on exactly how this happens. The Catholic Church teaches that most of us, when we die, are not yet ready to enter into Heaven. And so our souls go to another place, called Purgatory, where we work through the consequences of our sins. After a time in Purgatory, we are then given entrance into Heaven.

The esoteric teaching is similar, but there is one important difference. We believe that if a soul at death is not ready to enter into Heaven, it enters into a spiritual world, which is similar to Purgatory as mainstream Christians understand it. But after a certain time—perhaps a very long time—it returns to life on Earth to "try again" in another body. A part of every person's next life or incarnation will include working out the consequences of their sins in the previous life.

In practice, this amounts to much the same thing: Everyone agrees that most souls have not yet completed the work of spiritual development necessary to enter into Heaven, and that we need to spend a certain amount of time after death working out the consequences of our sins. But we disagree on exactly *where* we do this. You will hear me repeat over and over in this book that I don't plan to tell you what to believe about these things. You're an adult, and you can make up your own mind.

But let's return to the saints.

Every saint is set over some specific area of life on Earth. This can be a particular nation or ethnicity, as Saint Patrick is the patron of the Irish, Saint Andrew, the patron of the Scottish, and so on. It can be an occupation or way of life, as Saint George is the patron saint of soldiers and Saint Luke is the patron saint of doctors. It can even be something harmful, such as a natural disaster or disease. Saint Dymphna is called upon to help people struggling with mental illness; Saint Blaise protects against sore throats; and Saint Therese of Lisieux helps alcoholics.

In the way of thinking I am presenting in this book, these saints are humans who have achieved life on the Intellectual Plane. That means that they now participate in the governance of things on Earth.

In the traditional way of thinking, when we pray to a saint, we don't ask for their direct intervention. Instead, we ask for them to "pray to God for us." In the esoteric tradition, we see this as a metaphor. God's power is always creating reality, always pouring down the planes from even beyond the Plane of Unity. At the Intellectual Plane of existence, there is neither time nor space. And so when a saint "prays for us," it isn't the same as when we pray. They don't go into a separate room, light a candle, and hope that God is listening. They are immediately present to God. But each of them is also connected with that part of God's activities which ultimately goes on to create the things of this world of which that saint is a patron.

You can think of it as light passing through a prism. At the Plane of Unity, the light is colorless. The Prism is the Intellectual Plane. Here, the light appears to divide into a rainbow of many different colors. When the light hits a wall, one part will appear purple, another orange, another red, and so on. Of course, these colors aren't really separate; it's all one light. In our actual world, it's as though the "light" of God "divides" and creates the separate things that we experience, from a forest to a career as a doctor to the nation of Ireland. The saints are like particles which dwell in one particular ray of light. The great advantage of working with the saints is that they were human once, and so it is easy for us to understand them and for them to relate to us. When we pray to them, they help us attune ourselves to the particular "ray" of God, which is the "ray" that they themselves participate in. That is what we mean when we say the saints "pray for us." As such, we always close our prayers to the saints with the words "Pray for us," or, in Latin, *Ora pro nobis*.

Our Lady

As we have seen, the highest of the angels are exalted far beyond ordinary human beings, even beyond the universe itself! And yet, it is the teaching of the Christian tradition that one human being is set above even the highest of the angels. This is the Blessed Virgin Mary, called Queen of the Angels, and Queen of Heaven and Earth. We will discuss her in greater detail later on. For now, it's important to know that she is set above every other angel and saint. In magical terms, she is set at the summit of the Intellectual Plane. Perhaps she can even be said to be set above the Plane of Unity, at the unimaginable border between the Plane of Unity and the Infinity of God.

All of those things I am calling the "powers" or "energies" or "activities" of God are called graces, and Our Lady is given the power to dispense the graces of God wherever she sees fit. You will do very well indeed to cultivate a relationship with her if you do not already have one. Start today.

The intellect in man

As creatures on the Earth, all of us have only a very limited ability to experience the Intellectual Plane. However, we do have an intellect. Now, remember what we said above: by "intellect" we don't mean our ordinary thinking mind. We mean a higher mode of consciousness, which is capable of perceiving spiritual realities directly. In the Eastern Churches, this understanding has been better preserved than in the West. In Greek, the intellect is called the *Nous*, and it comes in for regular discussion by Orthodox writers and thinkers. Eastern Christians often call the *Nous* "the eye of the soul." In the West, this has been totally neglected for several hundred years. But the East has preserved the tradition of the *Nous*, and much of its practice is dedicated to clearing the *Nous* so that it may function properly. We will discuss this in more detail later on.

The Astral Plane

As we have seen, the Intellectual Plane is not actually the plane of thinking that we normally call "intellect." Instead, thought in the ordinary sense is part of the Astral Plane. In fact, the Astral Plane is the plane of all ordinary consciousness. Thought, imagination, dreams and visions, memory, emotion, and sensation are all part of the Astral Plane.

The Astral Plane is also the plane of spirits. This includes angels and saints. Their proper habitation is the Intellectual Plane, but when we encounter them we usually do so through the Astral Plane as a medium. This is because it is much easier for us to perceive the Astral Plane. The Astral Plane also includes ghosts, which are human spirits that are attached to the material plane for various reasons; nature spirits; and evil spirits such as demons. In this course, we won't be working with any of these.

Finally, the Astral Plane is a plane of subtle forces that shape human consciousness. This includes things like the seven planets of traditional astrology and the four elements of traditional physics. But it also includes the forces and cycles of history and culture that shape human life. A musical fad or a political movement, the sort that sweeps people up without them really being aware of it, is an Astral Plane phenomenon. It is an important teaching of the esoteric tradition that our minds aren't limited to our bodies. Instead, they are part of the Astral Plane, and each of us participates in many different group minds, all at once. Some of these large-scale Astral phenomena persist over time, such as the collective mind of a nation or culture. Some appear at specific moments, like tides, and recede again like the tides. If you've ever looked at a picture of yourself from 20 years ago and wondered what you were thinking wearing those clothes, which seemed so cool or trendy then but are now embarrassing, you've seen one of these Astral tides at work.

Regarding astrology: It's worth noting that many people think that astrology is forbidden to Christians, but this isn't true at all. Astrology can be defined as the belief that patterns on the Earth reflect patterns which can be seen in the Heavens, in the stars and planets. This allows us to predict certain trends on the Earth, but also to predict the movement of the stars and planets. This view is perfectly acceptable for Christians. What is forbidden is the belief that the planets and the stars *cause us to behave in certain ways, as though we had no free will.*

There are areas where I differ with the Catholic Church and other mainstream churches. As I've said above, I will try to be as upfront about these as possible throughout this course. But this is not one of those areas. No astrological event can force you to act in a certain way. What astrology predicts is patterns, rather like a weather forecast. But the weather doesn't force us to do anything. Some people become depressed in the wintertime, and most beaches empty out completely when a thunderstorm hits. But just a person who is affected by the winter weather can make use of special lamps to imitate sunlight and take Vitamin D supplements, we can always choose how we relate to the influences of the planets. The old saying among astrologers is that "A wise man is stronger than the stars."

Magical power is derived from the planes above the Astral, but the Astral Plane is primarily the plane on which magic operates. Remember our definition of magic: the art and science of causing changes in consciousness. All ordinary consciousness is Astral in nature.

Finally, while this model of the planes will work well for our needs, it should be noted that every plane can be divided even further. This is especially important with respect to the Astral Plane. The Astral Plane can be divided into Higher, Middle, and Lower levels. These correspond to different levels of consciousness. Ordinary waking consciousness and ordinary thoughts are largely of the Middle Astral Plane. This is the sort of consciousness you experience when you get out of bed, yawn, put on your slippers and make a cup of coffee. Above this, we have the Higher Astral Plane. This is the plane of higher forms of thought, and especially of spirituality and love. If, instead of simply rolling out of bed in the morning, you begin by saying a prayer, and then telling your spouse and your children good morning and that you love them, you begin your day by attuning yourself to the Higher Astral Plane. The Lower Astral Plane is the plane of negative thoughts and emotions, especially anger, fear, envy, uncontrolled lust and hatred. If you begin your day by being angry at the Sun for having risen and then immediately reaching for your cell phone to look at the latest bad news on Twitter, you begin your day by attuning yourself to the Lower Astral Plane. We're going to try not to do that.

The Energetic Plane

As I mentioned above, the Western world has only a limited understanding of this plane, but it is much discussed in other traditions. The Energetic Plane is the plane of subtle forces which maintain life on Earth and weave every life together. Have you ever felt "electrified" when walking into a crowd waiting for a concert to start? Or have you ever walked into a building and noticed that it had very "bad vibes," and perhaps afterwards felt depressed or simply "drained"? Those were experiences of the Energetic Plane.

There are many methods of working directly with the Energetic Plane, such as those taught in the traditions of yoga, qigong, and certain Asian martial arts. In this course, we will work with the energetic plane in two ways. First, you are encouraged to spend time every day in nature. Exposure to sunlight and fresh air, and the radiating energy of plants and natural features like rocks and rivers will strengthen your energetic body. Second, we will learn how to make use of certain natural substances such as incense, salt, and water, in order to benefit from their particular energies. Finally, some of the practices we will learn will allow Divine Power to descend down the planes of being to change the energy of certain objects, places—and ourselves.

The material plane

This is the plane of the ordinary matter that we experience. Not much more needs to be said about it. But it is important to note that everything in our material world is said to correspond to forces on the higher planes. This is where the traditions of astrology and of the four elements become useful, as they allow us to catalog the correspondences in ways that make sense to our minds. In an earlier time, Christians called this the "Great Chain of Being." Everything in the universe was thought to descend in an ordered way from God, through the ranks of angels and spirits, and down into the natural world of humans, animals, plants, and minerals.

The devil and evil spirits

Finally, it remains to say something more about the Devil, evil spirits, and evil magic. As noted above, these are all primarily phenomena of the Astral Plane, particularly the Lower Astral Plane. However, in another sense, the Devil and the demons are said to dwell at a level of being which is even below the material. This is what is meant when it is said that the Devil has been "cast into Hell." Notice that whenever we encounter the material world, we never encounter matter all by itself. It's always formed into an object, whether a blade of grass or a kitchen table. Natural objects are formed by God and have a natural life energy, as we've discussed. Man-made objects can be designed in ways to both purify their energetic environment and elevate the mind to the Higher Astral and even the Intellectual Plane, or they can pollute the energetic environment and cause us to descend to the Lower Astral. Or they can do nothing much at all.

In any case, every object that we encounter has some kind of order to it; that's why we are able to call it an object: a book, a candle, a cat, a blade of grass. Below this is what is sometimes called the Sub-Natural, or the level of Chaos. At this level of being, there is no order, no harmony, no pattern, no symmetry. The esoteric tradition teaches that, though the influence of the evil spirits extends as far as the Lower Astral Plane, their proper habitation is below even the material world, at the level of Chaos.

The Law of Correspondence

As discussed above, everything on the Material Plane corresponds to forces on the planes above it: Energetic, Astral, Intellectual and Divine. This is a major part of how magic works: On the material level, we can make use of natural objects or human artifacts which are attuned to specific influences on higher levels. For example, gold, sunflowers, frankincense, and the colors yellow and white are said to correspond to the Sun on the Astral Plane. The energy of the Sun and solar objects raises the vital spirits and restores health and enthusiasm. On the Intellectual Plane, the Sun is said to be governed by the Archangel Michael. On the Divine Plane, it is sometimes assigned to a certain name of God, usually Yahweh Elo'ah Ve'Da'ath, which is Hebrew for "God of Knowledge." (Please note: We don't mean a separate divine being named "the God of Knowledge," but rather God Himself as the God of Knowledge.) In order to bring solar influences into our life, we can combine all these things, including solar stones and frankincense, images of Saint Michael the Archangel, and calling upon God under the appropriate name.

It is important to note, however, that the Law of Correspondences isn't limited to astrology and applies whether or not you wish to make use of astrology. Every saint has their particular patronage, as we have seen. They also have their special attributes, which are special objects, natural substances, and colors associated with them. And, as we have seen, each also relates to a particular activity of God. Saint Therese of Lisieux, for example, is associated with roses. If you wish to form a relationship with her, you might set up a small shrine with an image of the saint and a rose flower, and burn some incense with rose in it, then say a special prayer associated with her. Remember that all prayer is ultimately directed to God, and when we close the prayer with "Pray for us" (*Ora pro nobis*), we call on that special divine current of which the saint is a conduit.

I
ADVENT

PART ONE

PREPARATION

Getting started

The following three sections will set the groundwork for the rest of this course. The first part covers the history and purpose of Advent in the Christian tradition, and goes over what supplies will be necessary for this course. The second part discusses fasting, a critical part of this course and of the Advent tradition. It gives suggestions on how to adapt the traditional fast to the needs and demands of modern life. The third part is perhaps the most important. It consists of a guide to Christian prayer and meditation and includes the outline for a private prayer ritual that we will use for the rest of the course.

CHAPTER ONE

The history and purpose of advent

Advent begins the Christmas season. The First Day of Advent is always a Sunday, and the markers of Advent are the four Sundays before Christmas. This means that Advent varies in length from year to year. If Christmas falls on a Sunday, the Advent season lasts four full weeks! On the other hand, if Christmas falls on a Monday, Advent is only three weeks long, plus the final Sunday.

This year, the First Day of Advent is today, November 28.

The name Advent comes from the Latin *adventus*, and means "coming." During the season of Advent, we are preparing for the coming of Christ into the world.

The world during Advent reflects the world prior to the coming of the Christ—it's cold and it's dark, and the powers of Nature are at their most hostile to human life. The Sun, that living icon of the power of the Most High God in the physical world, grows dimmer by the day, until it seems that Creation itself will be undone and the Chaos that was before the beginning will triumph over all.

In this dark season, we prepare our spirits for the hoped-for return of Light to the world. We do this through *fasting*, *prayer*, and *almsgiving*. We also prepare our homes for the Christmas season, and we celebrate certain seasonal customs that have come down to us from our ancestors.

How to prepare to celebrate Advent

You will need a few things in order to get the most out of this book. If none of the following is possible, you can still read this book and follow the practices to the best of your ability, but you'll get more out of it if you can spend a little bit of extra money and time to acquire the physical items listed. Remember that part of our goal is the re-enchantment of the material world; as such, it makes sense that we'll be using physical items as part of our practices!

The first thing that you will need is a space for prayer. The most basic requirements are simply a chair and a table. The chair should be solid and firm—a computer chair, couch, or even the side of your bed will do in a pinch, but something with a solid surface, like a wooden folding chair, is better.

The table is your altar. Now, it is worth noting that the term "altar" is more properly applied to a consecrated altar in a church, but at this time it is regularly used for a cleared space in a home which is set aside for religious objects and prayer. Ideally, you will have a permanent, standing altar in a part of your home reserved for this purpose. But again, don't let that requirement keep you from doing what you can—any flat space can serve as an altar, including the top of a dresser, a cleared space on a kitchen counter, a folding TV tray which can be taken down when you're done, even the top of a TV or entertainment center.

On your altar, you'll want certain items. At the very minimum, it should have a crucifix—this can either stand on the altar, lay flat upon it, or you can hang it on the wall directly above the flat surface. You will also want an image of the Blessed Virgin Mary, a candle, a container for holy water, and an incense burner of some kind. (I know that many people these days find it hard to tolerate incense; we will discuss some workarounds later.)

Saint cards and icons, flowers, cuttings from Christmas trees, Bibles or prayer books, additional lights, and any other religious items which help you feel a sense of connection to God are all appropriate for your altar.

All of the religious objects in question are known as *sacramentals*. This is a technical term for images and other physical objects which are meant as conveyors of a specific grace from God. We will be discussing a number of sacramentals in this book. For now, the most important thing to have is the crucifix; if you manage nothing else, make sure you have that.

You are also going to need an *Advent Wreath*. These wreaths and the set of four candles that go with them can easily be purchased online or in most Christian gift shops at this time of year. The wreath is going to symbolize our journey through Advent, and provide a focal point and a kind of time-keeper for our practice. We will discuss the Advent Wreath in detail at the end of this chapter.

Finally, make sure that you have a Bible, too. In this book, I have used a variety of translations for Scripture readings. The Epistles and Gospels for the Sundays in Advent are taken from the Douay-Rheims version, and the order of the readings is from the Latin Rite. Psalms invariably are taken from the King James Version, which is well-renowned for its beauty and has a long history of magical use in the English-speaking world. Other scriptural passages in the book come either from these or from the Revised Standard Edition, which I value for its clarity and accuracy. In your private reading, you can use whatever translation you like.

CHAPTER TWO

How to fast

Fasting and the Second Fall

Advent is traditionally a season of fasting and abstinence. In Catholicism, these are technical terms which have slightly different meanings. "Fasting" specifically means limiting the amount of food taken, while "abstinence" means limiting the type of food taken. Historically, the "fast" specifically meant that food should be limited to one 8-ounce meal per day, taken around noon. Two small snacks are also permitted, along with a bit of bread (without butter) and coffee in the morning if desired. The "abstinence" portion specifically means abstinence from meat. In practice, fasting and abstinence nearly always go together, and so we can use the term "fasting" as a catch-all.

These days, the Western churches do not impose a specific fasting requirement during Advent. This is, of course, a sign of their degradation, but it also presents an opportunity. There are many ways to fast, and the lack of a universal requirement allows us to experiment. But before we get to that, let's talk about the reason for fasting in the first place.

Fasting has two major purposes. The first is, quite simply, to withdraw our souls from the material world. The physical body is—to put it plainly—made out of meat. When the diet is limited to vegetable products, it becomes easier for the soul to focus on the non-physical world. This is why full-time veganism is practiced in those spiritual traditions that are especially interested in "getting off the planet" as quickly as possible, particularly various types of Buddhism and, in earlier times, Gnosticism and Pagan Neoplatonism.

The second purpose is to train the will. The desire for food is one of the functions of the lower part of the soul, called *Epithymia* in the traditional writings, or, in English "appetite." Appetite in this sense isn't limited to food, however. It also includes sexual desire, and, more generally, everything in our being that urges us toward physical pleasure, safety, and comfort. In the Christian tradition, the appetite isn't necessarily evil, but it has its proper place, and that place is under the firm control of the higher parts of the soul—the will and the reason.

As I wrote above, we don't have a specific fasting rule at this time, and that gives each of us a bit of latitude in coming up with one appropriate to our needs and situation in life. I'm going to suggest three possible levels of fasting, with different degrees of intensity; you're welcome to pick one of these, or come up with one of your own. First, though, we need to talk about another type of fasting.

The Second Fall

The following is a myth. It is not meant to be taken literally, but I hope you will take it seriously.

In the time of Jesus and his near-contemporaries, such as Plato and Gautama Buddha, the lowest level of reality on which human beings had their existence was the physical level, or the world of Nature. As such, the spiritual systems of the time focused on transcending physical reality. This is the reason for the rules of fasting and vegetarianism present in many of these traditions—as the material world was the lowest level of our existence, its transcendence was our immediate concern.

In the last few centuries, though, matters have gotten worse. Starting with the Industrial Revolution, accelerating with the Digital Revolution, and culminating in the advent of AI and virtual reality, humanity has undergone a Second Fall.

These days we spend most of our time not in Nature, and not withdrawn from Nature to a higher level of existence, but *below Nature.*

We sit in temperature-controlled rooms staring at illusions on screens, and the urges that bombard our appetites are not for food or sleep or even sex, but just for more screens—another "Like" on Facebook, another infuriating tweet, another level in a video game.

We have fallen from Nature to a level below Nature, the Sub-Natural.

The existence of such a plane of being is hinted at in certain esoteric writings, and what they suggest is troubling indeed. The old models of the world in which Heaven is above us and Hell below are metaphors meant to describe the environment we really inhabit in terms the human mind can grasp. The true Heaven is not above, but present to us all the time, if we can find it. Similarly, Hell is not below our feet—it is also around us and available to us, all the time. And the Sub-Natural, being below Nature, is not far from Hell.

In order to rise to Heaven, then, our task now is not merely to transcend the physical. We have to start by *returning* to the physical. For this reason, spiritual practices centered on Nature are especially appropriate for people in the modern world.

I therefore suggest that every fast should include an element of *fasting from technology*. This can be as simple as turning the phone and the computer off for the evening, or as advanced as spending a full day without using technology of any kind. Start where you're at, and start with what you can do.

Three levels of fasting

The traditional days for fasting are Mondays, Wednesdays, and Fridays. The modern Church limits such fasting as it prescribes to Fridays; more recent traditions have Wednesdays and Fridays. For our purposes, we can make Friday the main focus of our fasting, with Monday and Wednesday—or, for the seriously dedicated, the whole rest of the week—available to expand our practice as we grow in strength of will.

Here are three possible fasting regimens. All of these are meant to be suggestions. It may be that, rather than one specific regimen, a combination of two or three of them will work best for you. Again, it is far more important to pick something small that you can actually do than to pick something which is too big and will lead you to fail.

Level 1. On Fridays for the rest of Advent, eat a pescatarian diet (that is, only fish, no meat). Take no alcohol during these days, and do not snack between meals. After dinner, turn your cell phone off except for its call function—i.e., no apps or text messages—and turn the computer off as well.

Level 2. Follow all of the above practices, but add in Wednesdays. On Fridays, limit the diet to one small vegetarian meal of no more than 8 ounces of food. In addition, you may have two small snacks, and start your day with a piece of bread or a bagel without butter or cream cheese, and a hot drink of your choice. On Fridays, use no digital technology of any kind, unless you need to answer the telephone (with your voice). This means no TV either! Also on Fridays, after dinner, turn off all of the lights in your house, and spend the evening using only candlelight.

Level 3. Follow all of the above practices, but extend them to Mondays and Wednesdays as well. In addition, see if you can come up with one extra act of technological sacrifice. If you have a fireplace or wood-burning stove and your health and that of your family permit, see if you can go without running the heat one night of the week. If not, at least turn it down two or three degrees, or more. Wear a sweater and a cap instead. If you can possibly get away with it, do not drive anywhere during one of these days, or on Saturdays. One or more of these days, don't use any heat at all in the shower (this feels a lot better than you can imagine, once you get used to it).

Extra days

We will talk about this in due time, but you should know that the Wednesday, Friday, and Saturday following Saint Lucy's Day are special fasts known as Ember Days. Be prepared, that week, to add Saturday to your days of fasting!

CHAPTER THREE

Prayer and meditation

Prayer and meditation are the central features of the spiritual life. Many of us, today, either don't set time aside for prayer or don't even know how to pray in the first place. And while it's become common in recent years to discuss the supposed "health benefits" of meditation, few of us actually do it, and even fewer know that there are forms of meditation specific to the Christian tradition.

Prayer is the counterbalance to fasting. Fasting restrains the appetites and puts them under the control of the will and reason. But prayer puts the reasoning mind in touch with the Mind of God, and submits the personal will to the Will of God.

A guide to Christian Prayer and meditation

Every day we are going to pray and meditate, and we will also read certain devotional works. As we go on, we will discuss specific prayers, themes for meditation, and practices. The following is the guide that we will follow throughout this course. Be prepared to refer back to it as we go.

Section 1: Opening

Step 1. As soon as possible after rising, seat yourself in front of your altar. You should have some holy water present as well as incense. Begin by lighting a candle.

Step 2. Close your eyes, breathe in slowly and exhale fully. Make the sign of the cross slowly and reverently.

Step 3. With the same degree of reverence, pray the Our Father. Then pray the Hail Mary three times, and then finish with the Glory Be. Enter into each prayer, saying each word deliberately and with intention—not just uttering the syllables by rote. If there are any particular prayers or devotions to saints that you're personally working with, now is the time to pray them, with the same degree of deliberate intention.

The next two steps are optional, and you may use either or both. I encourage you to give both a try.

Step 4. Pick up the container of holy water, and say the following prayer.

> Cleanse me with hyssop, Oh Lord, and I shall be clean; wash me, and I shall be whiter than snow; have mercy on me, Oh Lord, according to Thy great mercy.

Or, if you prefer Latin:

> *Asperges me, Domine, hyssopo et mundabor; lavabis me, et super nivem dealbabor; misererei mei, Domine, secundum magnum misericordium tuum.*

Then sprinkle the holy water three times in each direction, turning clockwise: First, ahead of you, then to the right, then behind, then to the left.

Step 5. Pick up the incense in the same way, and say:

> Let my prayer be directed, Oh Lord, as incense in thy sight, the lifting up of my hands as an evening sacrifice.

If you prefer Latin:

> *Dirigatur, Domine, oratio mea, sicut incensum, in conspectu tuo: elevatio manuum mearum sacrificium vespertinum.*

Then, wave the incense three times in each direction, just as you did with the holy water.

Many people these days are unfamiliar and uncomfortable with the use of incense. For that reason, a simple guide to the use of incense has been included in the Appendixes.

Finally, stand in front of your altar or working table and raise your hands with the palms facing upward, in what is called the *orans* posture. Say the words:

> Our help is in the Name of the Lord,
> Who hath made the Heavens and the Earth.
> May the Lord be with me and guide my spirit in the work I am about to undertake.

Take some time to read over this opening and practice it until you can perform it from memory. We are going to use it regularly throughout the rest of this book.

Please note: The last line of the invocation may vary, depending on the work in question.

Section 2: Practice

This section will vary from week to week and day to day. The basic practice that we are going to engage in is called *lectio divina* or "divine reading," and consists of reading Scripture or some other devotional writing and meditating on the contents. However, as we go along, we will add in certain other practices.

To begin, Section 2 looks like this:

Step 1. Read. Begin by reading whatever text is provided for the day, which may be either a passage from the Bible or a story from the life of a saint.

Step 2. Remaining in a seated posture, take a few minutes to relax the muscles of your body, starting with your head and working your way down to your feet. Then take another minute or two to breathe deeply and rhythmically. Poised relaxation is the state you want to achieve.

Step 3. Bring to mind any idea that jumped out at you from your readings for the day, or another suitable theme for meditation—the season of the year, the meaning of Advent, the life of a saint whose feast it is are all appropriate. Spend 5–10 minutes thinking about this topic. Your mind will wander; when it does, just gently bring it back to your theme.

Section 3: Closing

Step 1. After your chosen time has run out (you can set a timer if you like) or after you've simply exhausted the possibilities of the theme you chose, it's time to bring your meditation to an end. The first thing to do is to pray. Pick a specific insight that came to you during your meditation—it could be a specific teaching of Our Lord, or an example of virtuous behavior from the life of a saint, or a virtue that you wish to develop. Or it could be a prayer of intercession for a loved one or someone else in your life. Or both. Either way, now is the time to add in a prayer to the Holy Spirit and to your Guardian Angel in your own words, asking to help apply the wisdom you gained during your meditation practice to your own life, especially in the day ahead of you.

Step 2. Close with a few more minutes of breathing. Then add a closing prayer—the Prayer of Saint Patrick, the Come, Holy Spirit Prayer, or the Prayer of Saint Francis are all good choices. (You can find all of these in the Appendixes of this book).

This is also a good time to add in prayers for any specific intentions you might have, either for yourself or others.

Step 3. Close with the Sign of the Cross, exactly as in the beginning.

If all this seems a little confusing, don't worry; we'll explain it in more exact detail as we go along.

CHAPTER FOUR

Charity

Finally, in addition to prayer and fasting, we should be prepared to engage in acts of charity during the Advent season. Together with fasting and prayer, charity or almsgiving forms a tripod, like a three-legged table that upholds the Christian life.

I'm not going to provide a detailed guide to charity. Everyone's circumstances are different, and only you know what you are able to give. If you have extra time, you can volunteer at a soup kitchen or a homeless shelter. If you work long hours and you have a young family, that's less likely—but you can probably give money, or you can donate food to a local food bank.

Be willing to be creative in your acts of giving. Did you notice how the first thing I suggested above was volunteering at a soup kitchen? That's because it was the first thing that I thought of, and it's the first thing that many people think of as well. But it isn't always the best option. Do you have a spare 100 dollar bill? Some night, go to a restaurant with the intention of leaving it as a tip for your server—no matter the bill and no matter the quality of service you receive. Is there a park or woodland near your home? Find a pair of gloves and a large garbage bag, go on a walk, and pick up every piece of litter you find. Is there someone you know who is lonely or struggling? Give them a call every week, or every day, during Advent, even if they annoy you.

I'll bet you can come up with a lot more ideas along these lines, if you spend a few minutes thinking about it. Don't tell anyone that you're doing these things, and don't get permission. Just do them.

The best guide to charitable giving is found in the first chapter of the Gospel of Luke:

> He looked up and saw the rich putting their gifts into the treasury; and he saw a poor widow put in two copper coins. And he said, "Truly I tell you, this poor widow has put in more than all of them; for they all contributed out of their abundance, but she out of her poverty put in all the living that she had." (Luke 21:1–4)

Do what you can and give what you have.

The Advent Wreath

The great symbol of Advent is the Advent Wreath. You can see a picture of it in the header of this post. An Advent Wreath is set with four candles: three are violet, and one is rose colored. Traditionally, every color has its own symbolism, and each station of the Wheel of the Year has its particular color. For now, two colors concern us.

- **Violet** is the color of suffering and penance. If that sounds unusual, consider that traditionally, it was viewed as a variant of black. These days, black is more or less a heavier version of violet. The three violet candles on the wreath symbolize Advent as a penitential season, reminding us that in these days we wander in darkness, waiting for the birth of the savior.
- **Rose** is the color of joy and happiness. There is one rose candle set amidst the violet candles, symbolizing hope for a renewed world and a reminder of the prophesied savior.

Notice the ratio here: We have three violet candles and one rose candle. This teaches us something about the nature of Advent. It is primarily a penitential season, but it is a joyous season as well—the trick is not to let the joyous element of the season overwhelm the penitential aspect. There will be time enough for celebration later.

Beyond the candles, every element of the Advent Wreath can be understood symbolically. The wreath itself is a circle, the symbol of eternity; the four candles symbolize the four elements of the world of matter, and their colors, the nature of life here below; the greenery is produced by sunlight manifesting in evergreen trees, symbolizing the eternal spirit dwelling in the world of matter; the fire slowly burning the candles away is the fire of time, drawing us inexorably upward toward the Eternal Fire which is God.

The Advent Wreath should be set at the dinner table or some other suitable location. Every Sunday, a new candle is lit. The first and second Sundays are violet, the third is rose, and the fourth is violet again.

The wreath itself should be blessed, and particular prayers are said every time a new candle is lit. Each Sunday in Advent will have its own chapter, and the proper prayers for each candle will be included in those sections.

Blessing for an Advent Wreath

This is our first proper magical working. It is designed to be as simple as possible. As you progress through this book, you will learn ways to expand and enhance it. Feel free to make use of those to expand this practice in the future.

On the other hand, you may find that even the simple blessing formula given here is too much for you. This is especially likely to be the case if you have young children who wish to take part in the blessing. It's much better to make use of a simple prayer that children can participate in and enjoy than an elaborate liturgy which bores them. In my own life, I've found that my 4-year-old daughter has no patience for the old Latin blessing before meals, which I love, but is very happy to lead everyone in singing a blessing she learned at her preschool.

We can define a "blessing" as a magical act whereby we call down power from the Holy Spirit in order to empower or "charge" an object, place, or a person. After this, the subject of the blessing is given the ability to transmit particular graces from God. It is worth noting that, in some magical traditions, spirits and even deities are *commanded* to perform certain favors for the magician. In Christian magic, this is never the case. The power that we work with is nothing other than the Holy Spirit of God Himself. That power is in no way subject to our control—but it can and does respond to our requests. That said, we should always know that our prayers have been answered and our intentions accomplished. As Our Lord Himself teaches us,

> Ask, and it will be given you; seek, and you will find; knock, and it will be opened to you. For every one who asks receives, and he who seeks finds, and to him who knocks it will be opened. Or what man of you, if his son asks him for bread, will give him a stone? Or if he asks for a fish, will give him a serpent? If you then, who are evil, know how to give good gifts to your children, how much more will your Father who is in heaven give good things to those who ask him! (Matthew 7:7–11)

Set your wreath in the place where it will remain for the Advent season—preferably the middle of your kitchen table. The candles should not be lit, but should be placed in their holders. You should have only as much light as you need to read the blessing; if you can memorize it ahead of time and perform the whole ceremony in darkness, that's even better.

You will also want some holy water; this can be obtained at most Catholic or Orthodox Churches. As always, if you don't have any particular ingredient, just leave it out. You can always take a normal cup of water, make the sign of the cross over it, and ask for God's blessing upon it. If it isn't as effective as water properly consecrated at a church, it isn't ineffective, either.

Make the Sign of the Cross, slowly and reverently. Say the Our Father, three Hail Marys, and the Glory Be.

If you have two participants, they should alternate the following section, with the person leading the rite as the reader. If you only have one person, they can do all the reading. When you see a +, make the sign of the cross over the wreath, visualizing it in the form of brilliant white light descending from Heaven above.

> Reader: Our help is in the name of the Lord.
> Response: Who hath made the Heavens and the Earth.
> Reader: Let us pray.
>
> Reader: Oh God, who made the Heavens and the Earth, we pray that you will pour down your blessings + onto this Advent Wreath. May it be a symbol of Eternity in Time, and of your presence in this valley of tears. Grant,

> Oh God, that as we await the coming of our savior on Christmas Day, that this wreath may guide our way, ever reminding us of your Justice, your mercy, and your love. Through Jesus Christ, Our Lord.

> Response: *Amen.*

The wreath is sprinkled with holy water.

Now, every time a candle is lit, it is accompanied by special prayers. As the candles are always lit on Sundays, these will be given in the section for each Sunday.

> Reader: Oh God, may your light shine on us and guide us throughout the Christmas season.

> Response: *Amen.*

PART TWO

FIRST WEEK OF ADVENT

CHAPTER FIVE

First Sunday in Advent

Welcome to the First Sunday in Advent!
Today, as we have already seen, the first, violet candle of the Advent Wreath is lit. Of course, you should attend Mass today if it is at all possible.

In addition, today we are going to begin our practice of prayer and meditation. Before you go on, refer back to the section entitled "Prayer and Meditation," and follow the steps given exactly. Before you start, make sure that you either have these memorized, or that you have the page bookmarked so that you don't have to waste your time flipping back and looking for it.

Readings for the First Sunday in Advent

Today's Epistle comes from the Letter to the Romans:

> Brethren, knowing the time, that it is now the hour for us to rise from sleep; for now our salvation is nearer than when we believed. The night is past, and the day is at hand; let us therefore cast off the works of darkness, and put on the armour of light. Let us walk honestly, as in the day; not in rioting and drunkenness, not in

chambering and impurities, not in contention and envy; but put ye on the Lord Jesus Christ.

Today's Gospel reading comes from the Gospel According to Saint Luke:

"There shall be signs in the sun, and in the moon, and in the stars; and upon the earth distress of nations, by reason of the confusion of the roaring of the sea and of the waves: men withering away for fear and expectation of what shall come upon the whole world. For the powers of heaven shall be moved; and then they shall see the Son of man coming in a cloud with great power and majesty. But when these things begin to come to pass, look up and lift up your heads, because your redemption is at hand." And He spoke to them a similitude: "See the fig tree, and all the trees; when they now shoot forth their fruit, you know that summer is nigh; so you also, when you shall see these things come to pass, know that the kingdom of God is at hand. Amen I say to you, this generation shall not pass away till all things be fulfilled. Heaven and earth shall pass away, but My words shall not pass away."

Meditation for the First Sunday in Advent

Today in your meditation, consider the various themes drawn from the readings and the symbolism of the first violet candle. In Saint Luke's Gospel, Jesus speaks of signs in the Heavens and upon the Earth. In the letter of Saint Paul, we are told that the hour has come; no longer should we slumber, nor engage in works of evil, but "put on the armor of the Light" and walk honestly, as in the day. As we light the first candle, we kindle a light in our homes to guide us during this season, and this light is a sign that the hour is at hand. The candle flame is an image of the Sun, and the Sun itself is an image of Christ, the Eternal Sun of the Spirit. Considering these and whatever other ideas may occur to you, enter into meditation.

May the Lord bless and guide you during this Advent season.

CHAPTER SIX

The Advent Wreath

Each candle on the Advent Wreath has its own special symbolism. Every Sunday, we will light a new candle, which will remain in use during the weeks to follow.

The first time you light a new candle, you may want to accompany it with the small ritual provided here, which includes a prayer and a Scripture reading. The readings are taken from the Psalms, and in every case the King James translation is used. There is an important reason for this. The Psalms have a very long tradition of magical use throughout the Christian world. Historically, all throughout Europe and elsewhere, specific Psalms were prayed for health, spiritual protection, fertility, and even to ward off natural disasters! In the English-speaking world, the King James translation of the Bible has been the preferred translation for magicians and traditional healers for many centuries. The selections from the Psalms given here are abbreviated. If you'd like to use the entire Psalm, you can find it in the Appendix, along with notes on its traditional uses.

The best time to light the Advent candles is at mealtime, and the following practice is written with that in mind.

As noted above, the candle has its own meaning. The first candle, which begins our Advent journey, symbolizes hope.

Step 1. We should always begin by making the Sign of the Cross, then praying the Our Father, three Hail Marys, and Glory Be. If you have young children whose attention may wander, you can simplify this; the sign of the cross will be enough. If you like, you may add in the sprinkling with holy water and censing with incense.

Step 2. Read the following short verse from the Psalm 23:

> The Lord is my Shepherd, I shall not want.
> He maketh me to lie down in green pastures.
> He leadeth me beside still waters.
> He restoreth my soul.
> Surely goodness and mercy will follow me all the days of my life, and I shall dwell in the house of the Lord forever.

Step 3. Pray:

> Oh God, as we light this candle, may it be for us a symbol of the Eternal Light of Thy Holy Spirit, and a sign of hope for we who wander in the darkness of the lower world. *Amen.*

Light the candle.

During the meal that follows, you can encourage every member of your family to talk about hope; something they hope for; what hope means to them. What does it mean when we say that "hope" is a virtue? What should we hope for? You can also take hope as a theme for your meditations in the week to come.

CHAPTER SEVEN

Advent and the Second Coming

The Second Coming

As we've discussed, Advent means "coming." During Advent, we remember and re-live the First Coming of Christ. But we also prepare for his Second Coming—which is the theme of the Gospel reading for the First Sunday.

Now, it's probably the case that modern Christians, particularly if they are of the esoteric bent, either don't think about the Second Coming much or don't want to think about it. But there really is no getting around it—it's a central part of the Christian tradition as a whole, and a central part of Advent in particular. In the Christian tradition, Jesus is coming again, at an hour unknown to us, to judge the living, and the dead, and the world by fire.

So let's talk about the end of the world.

The final judgment

Apocalypse 20:11–15 states:

> And I saw a great white throne, and him that sat on it, from whose face the earth and the heaven fled away; and there was found no place for them.
>
> And I saw the dead, small and great, stand before God; and the books were opened: and another book was opened, which is the Book of Life: and the dead were judged out of those things which were written in the books, according to their works.
>
> And the sea gave up the dead which were in it; and Death and Hell delivered up the dead which were in them: and they were judged, every man according to his works.
>
> And Death and Hell were cast into the lake of fire. This is the second death.
>
> And whosoever was not found written in the Book of Life was cast into the lake of fire.

Myth and the Christian tradition

The perspective of this book is that the Bible is myth, and the Christian tradition must be understood mythically. Before you panic, we should discuss precisely what that means.

According to an ancient definition, myths are stories of things that *never happened*, but *always are*. Pay attention to that definition, it will be important as we go on. Appropriately enough, it can be read in several different ways. In one sense, it's saying that even if a myth didn't actually happen, it's a story in which we can find meaning and which teaches us something important about life.

On a deeper level, it's saying that a myth is a story which expresses a fundamental principle of nature, human life, or reality itself in a form—a story—the human mind can grasp. On still another level, it reveals one of the great truths of our magical philosophy.

Myths "never happen," but "always are." In order for something to "happen," it has to take place in the world of Time. But at the highest levels of being, there is no such thing as time. God is eternal. We usually take the word "eternity" to mean "a very long time," but that isn't right. Eternity actually means *outside of time*.

After God, there are other things which are outside of time—the patterns which shape the world of time itself. We technically call these patterns "aeviternal," to distinguish their existence from the true Eternity of God Himself. Aeviternal things never happen, because they are not found in the world of Time. They are found in the world of Being, and they always *are*.

Now, here is the tricky part. The claim of the Christian religion is that its central myth, that of the life, death, and resurrection of Jesus Christ, is not only myth but is also history.

There are two possible ways to understand this. For some, and especially for many modern people, Jesus's story can be understood as simply myth. This doesn't make it any less meaningful, and in fact can make it even more meaningful.

But for most Christians, and for nearly all Christians (with exceptions) throughout history, the story of Christ is both history and myth at once. The famous English novelist C.S. Lewis, once he was convinced by his friend J.R.R. Tolkien of the truth of the Christian religion, expressed this perspective beautifully in a letter to Arthur Greeves:

> Now the story of Christ is simply a true myth: a myth working on us in the same way as the others, but with this tremendous difference that it really happened: and one must be content to accept it in the same way, remembering that it is God's myth where the others are men's myths: i.e., the Pagan stories are God expressing Himself through the minds of poets, using such images as He found there, while Christianity is God expressing Himself through what we call "real things."

I personally believe this, but I make no demands on the beliefs of my readers. The point I want to make is simply this: When we understand the teachings of the Christian tradition mythically, and then apply them as guides to spiritual practice, they become our guide to the whole of Christian magic. This is what is meant by the "esoteric" tradition—not mixing Christianity with ideas from other traditions, but understanding the inner side of Christianity as it is.

How to understand the Second Coming esoterically— and how to misunderstand it

Here is how this perspective applies to the Second Coming: If myths never happened, but always are, then the end of the world is something that is always happening. On some level, we all know this. The only constant in our world under Heaven is change. Think of your own life—Is it different now from the way it was ten years ago? One year ago? How about a month ago? How about last week? I bet if you think about it, it isn't even the same as it was an hour ago.

Sometimes the changes that we're talking about are very big. I have friends and loved ones who were alive ten years ago but are no longer with us today; on the other hand, I have other friends whom I have not yet met, and family members who have not even been born! And I'll bet you do too.

Now, all change is an ending. The places, people, habits, thoughts, and emotions, even the larger cultural patterns that characterize our world, and that in a sense truly are our individual worlds: All of these are changing, and ending, all the time. All change is a kind of death, a kind of apocalypse.

The mystic traditions of the East refer to this constant process of change and dissolution as *anicca*, or impermanence. The awareness of *anicca* is a central feature of many Eastern systems of spiritual development. The proper response to *anicca* is detachment from impermanent things, which is to say, from all things. Attachment leads to *dukkha*, or suffering. This must necessarily be the case, as all the objects of our attachment are always melting away, always dying.

Now, many Eastern systems stop at this point, framing the goal of the spiritual life as the awareness of *anicca* and the release from attachments in general. In the West, we have always had a different approach. The Western Mysteries say that, yes, everything in the world of Becoming is characterized by *anicca*, impermanence, but there is a world beyond the world of Becoming. This is the world of *Being*, which is permanent. The correct objects of our attachment are not the illusory things of the world of Becoming, but the real things of the world of Being. Above all else, the correct object of our attachment is God, Father, Son, and Holy Spirit.

It's actually more correct to say that there are many worlds beyond the world of Becoming, each a little more stable, solid, and permanent. Above, beyond, beneath, and upholding it all is the Eternal One, God Himself, that absolute permanence beyond even Being itself, by which all the worlds are held together, and from which the great fire of existence constantly pours through creation.

We say that Christ is returning. For those who are ready, his arrival will be as the arrival of the bridegroom at his wedding feast.

For those who are not ready, his coming will be as the coming of a thief in the night.

This is not meant to terrify us; God isn't an abusive father coming home to beat us up if our room isn't clean. These images are tools, and they are meant to teach us. How do we live, and who do we become, if we live in the awareness that Christ could return at any moment? If, at any moment, the Book of Life will be opened, and will we be judged according to our deeds? How do we live, knowing that the end is always here, and the Book of Life is never closed?

The unpredictable apocalypse

There are some ends-of-the-world scenarios that we can predict. Cycles of historical change have been discovered by historians as well as philosophers and magicians. We can see them coming, have a sense of their general shape and tenor, and plan accordingly. William Strauss and Neil Howe accurately predicted that a generational crisis was coming to America in our time, way back in 1996. Now, no one knew the exact shape the crisis would take—and we still don't, as it is still unfolding, all around us. In the same way, nobody in the middle of September knows exactly what winter will be like that year. Will it be long and cold, snowy and wet, or warmer than usual? We can't know that in advance, but we can know that winter will come, and prepare accordingly.

There are other apocalypses that cannot be predicted. You never know when a sudden economic downturn will put you out of work, or a natural disaster will render large parts of your state or country uninhabitable. You never know when you'll get that phone call telling you that someone you love has died. The only way we can prepare for these crises is by maintaining ourselves in a constant state of readiness, by forming and maintaining conscious contact with God, and the Heavenly World of His angels and saints.

The end has already come

There is still another way to understand the Second Coming.

Above, we described the Intellectual Plane, and we said that it was the natural habitation of the angels of God—and also of the saints, those holy men and women who have transcended material embodiment.

Now, time is primarily a feature of the Physical Plane. It is here that events follow one another in sequence, one thing leading to the next, everything always becoming, nothing permanently enduring. It is also a feature of the Astral Plane, but here it becomes much more variable: Think of the way that time passes in a dream.

The Intellectual Plane is beyond time. If the saints dwell there, then they dwell beyond time, in eternity. For the saints, then, according to the esoteric tradition, the end of the world has already come, and they dwell even now in the kingdom of God.

A word to the wise

By the way—never doubt that the end of the world could also simply happen, exactly as your Catholic grandma or your fundamentalist neighbor thinks it will. If the last few years haven't taught you that you have no idea what's really going on in the world, you haven't been paying attention. And besides that—it's the central claim of the Christian religion that, at a particular moment in time, the world of myth erupted into the world of history. This is the life, death, and resurrection of Jesus Christ. Did it really happen as a historical event? As I said, I think that it did, though I also think it's far more important to understand it as myth than as history. That said, if it can happen once, it can happen again.

The Second Coming meditation

During Advent, we unite ourselves with the changing tides of Nature in order to prepare our spirits for the return of Christ.

On Fridays during Advent, perform the following meditation.

Preparation. Set up your altar or working table as you have been instructed. At a minimum, you should have a crucifix and an image of Mary, a candle, and containers for holy water and incense.

Step 1. Perform the opening, as described above.

Step 2. Return to your seat, and make a profession of faith suitable for you and your practice. You will find several different options in the Appendix to this book.

Step 3. Now is the time to make a humble confession of your sins. When doing so, remember the purpose of Confession. It is not to harm us. It is to heal our souls: First, by removing any foreign element; Second, restoring the soul to its original wholeness; and Third, re-aligning the soul with the path of spiritual evolution whose summit is God Himself.

You can do this simply by calling to mind your sins, and then saying one of the Confiteor prayers, which you will find in the appendixes to this book. Afterwards, take a moment to imagine a current of holy fire descending from Heaven. Imagine it pouring into you, burning away the black impurities of sin, and restoring you to wholeness.

Step 4. Take your seat and enter into meditation as you have been instructed, first taking time to relax your body and still your energy with a few minutes of rhythmic breathing.

Then, call to mind the images from the Book of Revelation from the beginning of this chapter. See the return of Christ; imagine it happening tomorrow, or next week—or right now. Imagine the Book of Life being opened, and your deeds read out before the assembly of Heaven and Earth. Who are you, at this moment? How have your actions shaped your present life? Who were you intended to be? What place have your works in this life merited for you in the next?

Remember that the "next life" is a term with many meanings. It means the eternal fate of your immortal spirit, once all of time is over and done. If you believe in reincarnation, it means your next life in this world, which will allow you to work out the consequences of your actions in this life and learn from any mistakes you may have made and failed to correct. It means the life that you will live from the moment you get up from your meditation chair and begin the rest of your day. Who will you be? Who are you meant to be?

Call to mind that healing, divine fire that descended during the Confession. Who will you be—now that you have been restored to wholeness and the grace of God?

Take a moment to visualize the best possible outcome for all of the various next lives that you will live. Pray that it may be so, and ask for the guidance of your Guardian Angel. Pray that, as the austerities of Advent prepare you for the coming of the Christmas season, so too you may be willing to suffer what you must in this life, for the sake of the next. This is also a good time for any other particular prayers or devotions you may want to add.

When you are ready, return for a few minutes to simple, rhythmic breathing, awareness of the Presence of God.

Step 5. Close your meditation as you have been instructed.

CHAPTER EIGHT

The Guardian Angel

As we discussed in the chapter on magical philosophy, each of us has a Guardian Angel. These are powerful spirits sent by God to watch over and guide us in this life. No matter who you are or where you are at in life, you will do well to cultivate a relationship with your Guardian Angel. This is especially true if you are undertaking a new form of magic or spiritual development—as you are!

Working with your Guardian Angel falls under the tradition of angel magic. Angel magic is a very broad topic, and in this course we'll only scratch the surface of it. Let's begin by learning a simple ritual for contacting our guardian angels.

Preparation. Set up your altar or working table. At minimum you should have a crucifix and a candle. You will also want an image of a Guardian Angel. This can be a statue, a prayer card, or an icon. All of these are easy enough to find, but if you really can't find one, you can find a picture online and print it out. (If you do this, be careful not to put the paper anywhere near the candle, as it will easily catch fire.)

Step 1. Take a seat, relax your body, and take a few deep breaths.
Step 2. Make the sign of the cross, slowly and reverently.
Step 3. Pray the Our Father, three Hail Marys, and the Glory Be.

Step 4. Turn your attention to the image of the angel, and say the Guardian Angel Prayer:

> Angel of God, my guardian dear,
> To whom God's love commits me here
> Ever this day (or night) be at my side
> To light, and guard, and rule, and guide.

Step 5. Talk to your angel. Tell him that you'd like to get to know him better. Tell him about this course of study that you're beginning, and what you hope to get out of it. Ask him to help and guide you on your magical journey. Tell him anything else you like.

Step 6. Close your eyes, relax your body, and let go of any thoughts. Be aware that your angel is present with you. You may find that certain thoughts, images, or direct messages come into your mind now. In some cases, you may even find yourself in a conversation with your angel.

Step 6.a. If your angel or any spirit appears to you, you should always test it. The traditional method for this is to ask the spirit, "In the name of Jesus Christ Our Lord, do you confess the coming of Christ in the flesh?" If it answers "Yes," you may proceed with the conversation. If not, then, in a firm voice, tell it, "In the name of Jesus Christ, be gone from this place at once."

Step 7. Return to rhythmic breathing for a time. When you are ready, slowly open your eyes, and perform the complete closing as you have been instructed. In addition to the usual closing prayer, you may wish to repeat the Guardian Angel Prayer and perhaps say the Saint Michael Prayer, as he is the prince of the Heavenly Host.

You will want to write down any thoughts or ideas that came to you to refer back to later on.

Two more notes about angels. In the ritual above, I've referred to your Guardian Angel as "he" and "him." But this isn't really accurate—angels are bodiless spirits, and they don't have gender as human beings do. In artwork, they are sometimes depicted as female, sometimes as male. This seems to reflect the reality that some of them "feel" masculine, and others "feel" feminine. You can refer to your own Guardian Angel as he, she, or it.

It's also worth pointing out that it is not only individuals who have guardian angels. As we discussed in the chapter on magical philosophy, families, towns, and entire nations have guardian angels. So do churches, organizations, and natural places like national parks and forests. The guardian angels for groups and larger institutions typically come from the higher choirs of angels, the archangels and principalities.

The simple formula given above can be used to contact any angel or saint.

CHAPTER NINE

Saint Andrew's Day

We now come to our first Saint's Day in Advent, which is the Feast of Saint Andrew.

Now, please note: Saint Andrew's Day is November 30. As we've seen, Advent can begin on any day between November 27 and December 3. That means that during some years, Saint Andrew's Day will fall during Advent, but some years it won't! Please note: If the Feast of Saint Andrew doesn't fall during Advent during the year when you're using this book, that's no reason not to celebrate. There are practices associated with Saint Andrew that you may find immensely helpful—whether or not his Feast Day happens to fall after Advent Sunday this year.

Saint Andrew is a very versatile saint. Many know him as the patron saint of Scotland, but his patronage extends well beyond Scotland and the Scottish diaspora. Among places, his patronage also includes Barbados, Georgia, Ukraine, Romania, Greece, Russia, and Cyprus. And among people, he watches over fishermen, rope-makers, textile workers, singers, miners, pregnant women, butchers, and farm workers, as well as both the Russian Navy and the United States Army Rangers (let us hope that they never come into conflict, and the saint be forced to choose!) Finally, perhaps due to his day falling in the season of winter with its many ailments, he is invoked for protection against sore throats, fever, and the whooping cough.

Originally, of course, Saint Andrew was one of Jesus's disciples. In fact, he was the first disciple. In the Gospel according to Saint John, we learn:

> The next day again John was standing with two of his disciples; and he looked at Jesus as he walked, and said, "Behold, the Lamb of God!" The two disciples heard him say this, and they followed Jesus. Jesus turned, and saw them following, and said to them, "What do you seek?" And they said to him, "Rabbi" (which means Teacher), "where are you staying?" He said to them, "Come and see." They came and saw where he was staying; and they stayed with him that day, for it was about the tenth hour. One of the two who heard John speak, and followed him, was Andrew, Simon Peter's brother. He first found his brother Simon, and said to him, "We have found the Messiah" (which means Christ). He brought him to Jesus.

Traditional celebrations

Saint Andrew is the patron saint of Scotland, and—after the usual way with these things—he is celebrated both in Scotland itself and by Scottish descendants the world over. These celebrations are marked by food, music, beer, and Scottish heritage generally. In the town of Saint Andrews itself, the party continues for a week!

In Romania, which is also one of Saint Andrew's many charges, Saint Andrew's Day has a particular association with wolves. On this day, wolves are able to talk, and, of course, they may eat all that they like. Romania also preserves a very interesting magical practice on Saint Andrew's Day. Early in the morning, Romanian mothers go into the garden and gather tree branches, above all from flowering trees such as apples and cherries. A bunch of branches is made for each member of the family. Whoever's tree branches bloom into flowers by New Year's will be blessed with health and good fortune throughout the year.

The night before Saint Andrew's Day—Saint Andrew's Eve—is also a traditional time for magic, witchcraft, and divination. In many parts of Europe, Saint Andrew's Eve was known as the time when witches, vampires, and other evil spirits began to prowl the Earth. Such traditions are very common the world over. The darkness of winter, when the light of the sun is faint and life withdraws from the world of nature, is the time when spirits are abroad in the land.

Fortunately, Saint Andrew's Day has given us another tradition, that of the Saint Andrew's Cross. Saint Andrew himself met his death by being crucified upon a cross turned on its side, so that it forms the shape of an × rather than a + plus sign. This Saint Andrew's Cross, with or without the image of the saint upon it, is traditionally placed over fireplaces and windows in order to prevent evil spirits from entering the home.

Finally, one of the very finest traditions of Saint Andrew's Day is the Saint Andrew Christmas Novena. This is a very beautiful, powerful, and, in my experience, effective prayer. Instructions will be provided in the next section.

Suggestions for practice

This section will be included as part of the discussion for every saint's day from here on out. All of the ideas given here are suggestions; you are more than welcome to modify them or ignore them entirely. If you do a bit of research, you're guaranteed to find additional traditions that I haven't mentioned—and of course, you're always welcome to come up with something totally new!

Here are a few possibilities for celebrating the Feast of Saint Andrew:

1. **A Day of Scottish Heritage.** If you are Scottish, or if you have any Scottish ancestry and you're interested in connecting with it, today is the day for you! Scottish music, traditional food and drink, games and entertainment can all be part of your celebration today.
2. **Divination.** You are, of course, welcome to try any of the traditional methods of divination mentioned here. You don't have to be Romanian to gather branches from your apple trees, if you have any. Alternatively, you might like to use this day to work with a traditional divination oracle such as the tarot or horary astrology.

    We will discuss divination in more detail on Saint Lucy's Day below.
3. **Meditation.** Today, consider taking some aspect from the traditions of Saint Andrew as a theme for meditation. You might contemplate

the Gospel account of his being called by Jesus, or you could consider some of the legends that have grown up around him. Or place an image of him, with or without the Saint Andrew's Cross, on your altar, and simply contemplate it as a theme for meditation. What does it mean to be crucified in this way?

The Saint Andrew novena

A novena is an extended period of prayer, usually lasting nine days. The Saint Andrew novena is different, as it is prayed from this day until Christmas. It is a simple prayer, but many can attest to its miraculous powers, myself very much included. To pray the novena, follow these steps:

Preparation. The first time you say this prayer, you should do so in your temple space, with your altar set up as described previously. In addition to the usual implements, you may want to include an image of Saint Andrew. After the first day, you can dispense with the opening ritual. You should still begin with the sign of the cross, the Our Father, and the Hail Mary, but after that you can proceed directly to step 3. When practicing outside of your temple, you can say the prayers anywhere you like, even while driving (if you can do so safely), sitting on a bus or in a waiting room, and so on.

Step 1. Perform the complete opening, as you have been instructed.

Step 2. Recite the following words:

> Hail, and blessed be the hour and moment at which the Son of God was born of a most pure Virgin at a stable at midnight in Bethlehem in the piercing cold. At that hour vouchsafe, O my God, I beseech thee, to hear my prayers and grant my desires.

Now, name your desire. I find that it is very helpful to use affirmative statements at this point and go into detail. Rather than saying, "I wish to get a new job," say,

> By the power of God, I ask that by this time next year I will be employed full-time at a job in my field which allows me to cover all my expenses, grow in my career, and have the leisure time I need to enjoy life with my family.

Continue with:

> Through Jesus Christ and His most Blessed Mother.
> Amen.

Step 3. Now comes the hard part: Repeat Step 2 *15 times a day*, every day, from today until Christmas Eve. Yes, every day.

Now, we all know that life is busy and complicated. If you can't get all 15 prayers said in one sitting, simply *break them up throughout the day*. Maybe you have time for only three repetitions in the morning. That's fine; say it six more times on your drive to work and six more times coming home. The saints are smart. They'll get the message.

Step 4. Perform the closing, or, after the first day, conclude with the Sign of the Cross.

CHAPTER TEN

The Christmas Tree

The Christmas Tree is the best-known symbol of the Christmas season. These days, most Americans, from what I can tell, put up their tree as soon after Thanksgiving as they can manage, and light and decorate it that day. Traditionally, this was not done; the tree would be put up near Christmas and not lit or decorated until after Mass on Christmas Eve. Certainly, that was the custom in my family, but especially if you have young children, you may find it hard to buck the trend. That's all right—I myself usually take my children to cut down a tree at a local farm the week after Thanksgiving, and decorate it that day.

As with the Advent Wreath, the tree can be understood on many different levels. Let's discuss a few of them now.

The tree is the mightiest creature in the plant kingdom; it stands in relation to herbs and vegetables as humans do to animals. In the forest, every tree becomes a kind of world unto itself, providing a living space for hundreds of creatures, from insects to birds and mammals. As such, it is a symbol of the entire world of Nature which has been created by God, and even of the cosmos beyond our world. In many traditional cosmologies, our world is one of many, all of which hang from a single great tree. In Western esotericism, it is the Tree of Life, the great symbol of the unfolding process of creation.

Like all green plants, trees turn sunlight into energy. In this way, they literally turn sunlight into their own bodies. As we eat of their fruits, or of the flesh of animals who have eaten of them, we then turn that sunlight into our own bodies. The Sun Himself is a visible icon of the Hidden Sun of the Spirit, which is Christ. As the body of Christ nourishes our spirits, the body of sunlight, which is all plant and animal food, nourishes our bodies.

The Christmas Tree is always an evergreen, usually a fir or a spruce. As its leaves stay green even in the darkest months, we are reminded of the Eternal Reality of God, and of the eternal Presence of God, which can guide us even in the darkest times.

You can and should use the practice of meditation to go deeper with any of these ideas and explore new ones, whether from traditional sources or your own personal inspiration.

How to use real trees responsibly

Our world needs more trees in it, not fewer, and so many people prefer an artificial tree to a real one. If that's the case for you, you can still use the material in this section. The artificial tree still expresses the symbolic ideas, and it can still be ritually blessed, as described below.

I personally prefer real trees, though; it's quite simply the case that a living tree has power, as in magical power, that an artificial tree does not and cannot have. But a tree is a living being. Apart from any environmental concerns, that means it must be treated respectfully, just as an animal must be treated respectfully. Let's talk about how to do that.

Cut down your own tree

If at all possible, find a farm in your area that allows you to cut down your own tree. This has a great number of advantages. First, you're supporting local agriculture, and putting your money and time into your local economy and the land where you live. Second, it allows you to put your energy into the tree from the very beginning. You find the tree yourself, and you do the work of cutting it down and hauling it to the barn to pay for it. By doing this, you mix your energy, which is the very substance of your body, with that of the tree. That's very important on an esoteric level, as we'll discuss presently.

Understand you are working Alchemy

Here is one of the great secrets of magic: *We are all doing magic all the time.*

As long as we are living, conscious beings, we are participating in changes in consciousness, and doing so in accordance with *some will*.

Now, that branch of magic by which physical things are transformed and led to express their hidden spiritual nature is known as *Alchemy*. Usually, when we hear that word, we picture medieval wizards working in secret laboratories in high towers under the Moon. But Alchemy, like magic as a whole, is something we practice all the time. Every act of cooking is a work of Alchemy, and every cook is an alchemist. This is a secret that good cooks as well as good psychics know—every meal contains a trace of the person who prepared it. Eat a meal cooked in a filthy kitchen by someone who hates you and doesn't want to be doing the work, and you'll feel it, if you have the least bit of sensitivity; eat a meal made with love in a clean and happy kitchen by a cook who cares about their work, and you'll feel that too.

In just the same way, the process of taking a tree from nature and transforming it into a living symbol of the Christmas season is a great work of Alchemy. As such, it must be undertaken with the greatest care. Before you even leave the house, take a few minutes to still your mind and say a prayer. You can ask Saint Francis, as patron of ecology, or the archangel Uriel, as the archangel who governs the Earth element, to guide you in your day's work. Play Christmas music in the car on the way to the farm—good Christmas music, the kind that inspires you and invokes the Spirit of the Season. (For me, in an ideal world, that would mean something like the Renaissance composer Adrian Willaert's Christmas Vespers. Since my wife and kids have to share the car with me, Frank Sinatra's 1948 Christmas album works well enough!)

Now, don't stress about maintaining the right mood or the right attitude—that's the best way to make sure you won't! Just do the prayer to the best of your ability and aim to enjoy yourself, but also to act in the spirit of the Christmas season, and to invoke the divine to guide your actions.

Bless your tree

When you find your tree, talk to it. Tell it your intention—"I'm cutting you down to place you in my house. You will be covered in lights, and be a symbol of joy and an icon of the Great World Tree itself."

I like to carry a water bottle with me, filled with water or something else—wine is traditional, but coffee will do, and hot chocolate might be even more appropriate—so that I can surreptitiously pour out an offering to the spirit of the land. Actually, I do this anywhere I go hiking. It's worth noting that an offering like this is in no sense an act of "worship," any more than handing a glass of water to a friend is an active worship. That said, don't do this if it feels inappropriate or if you believe that it violates the teachings of your Church.

When you get the tree home, bless it. The United States Conference of Catholic Bishops provides a functional blessing ceremony on their website, which you can use as is or modify. I personally prefer to use more complex methods of ceremonial magic to invoke divine light into the tree. A simple blessing ceremony, which can be practiced by anyone, is provided below.

A simple blessing ceremony

For this ritual, all you need is yourself and your tree. If you want, you can provide yourself with holy water and incense. Before the tree, make the Sign of the Cross, and then pray the Our Father, Three Hail Marys, and Glory Be, as we've discussed.

If you have holy water, hold it aloft and say the words, "Cleanse me with hyssop, oh Lord, and I shall be clean; wash me, and I shall be whiter than snow; have mercy on me, Oh God, according to thy great mercy." Then sprinkle holy water in the four corners of the room, three times each.

If you have incense, hold it aloft and say the words, "Let my prayer be directed, O Lord, as incense in thy sight, the lifting up of my hands as an evening sacrifice." Wave the incense three times in each quarter of the room.

If you have two participants, they should alternate the following section, with the person leading the rite as the reader. If you only have one person, they can do all the reading. When you see a +, make the sign of the cross over the tree, visualizing it in the form of brilliant white light descending from Heaven above.

      Reader: Our help is in the name of the Lord.
      Response: Who hath made the Heavens and the Earth.
      Reader: Let us pray.

      Reader: Oh God, who made the Heavens, and who made the Earth to bring forth vegetation, and the tree to bring forth the fruit of its kind, we pray for your blessing + be upon this Christmas Tree. Let your divine light fill it, that it may bring light, and joy, and peace to our home during this Christmas season. Let it be a visible reminder to us of the gifts of Nature and of the reality of the Life Eternal during this time of cold and darkness. Let its spirit be blessed, and may the blessing of Almighty God bring fertility to the soil and the land where it was grown and peace and prosperity to the people of that land. Through Jesus Christ, Our Lord.

      Response: *Amen.*

The tree is sprinkled three times with holy water, and censed three times with incense.

      Reader: We thank thee, O Lord, for the gift of this tree. May thy blessing be upon it and radiate through our home during this Christmas season.

      Response: *Amen.*

Close with the Sign of the Cross.

Use your tree!

Whatever you do, do not be one of those people who throw the tree out on the curb on December 26. In the first case, it should stay up and lit through Epiphany, on January 3. But more to the point, you should not throw it out at all. Every part of your tree can and should be used.
    But how?

Many different ways. You can toss a handful of twigs and needles into a pot of water on the stove and bring it to a boil; let it go all day, and it will fill your house with the scent of evergreen. Or boil for a few minutes to make a tea which is both tasty and rich in Vitamin C. You can use dried-out twigs with needles as incense—be careful with this, as the needles will burn *very* quickly. And at the end of the season, you can chop it into firewood. I like to burn the very last of the Christmas tree on Candlemas, which is the true finale of the Christmas season.

As odd as it sounds, you can also eat your tree. A fine recent book entitled *How to Eat Your Christmas Tree* discusses this in detail. It is included in the recommended reading in the Appendix. At minimum, you should consider making at least one round of Christmas Tree Tea—this is a way of bringing the magical energies of the tree directly into your body and spirit.

CHAPTER ELEVEN

Foundations of Christian Magic: The Sign of the Cross

The use of the cross as a protective symbol is well known and attested from the earliest days of Christianity.

Long ago, there was a sorcerer named Cyprian who fell in love with a Christian woman, a virgin named Justina, and desired to possess her. Cyprian was a great wizard who had learned all the sorceries of the ancient world, and he cast a love spell on Justina. But Justina made the Sign of the Cross, and Cyprian's magic fell apart. Cyprian tried it again, and again, but every time Justina made the Sign of the Cross, and Cyprian's spells came to nothing. Ultimately, Cyprian gave up working with evil magic and became a Christian.

Of course, the power of the cross to repel evil is well known from a thousand sources. In horror movies, it's common for a character to hold up a cross in order to repel a vampire, only for the vampire to laugh evilly and brush it aside with some line like "You expect your pitiful faith to save you? I am Filmstupidus, the attractive movie vampire, and crosses do not scare me!"

Real life, of course, is quite different. The Sign of the Cross puts us directly into contact with God and invokes his power into us, cascading through the worlds of being from the eternal spiritual realm down to our physical world. We can use the sign of the cross as a protective ritual, exactly as Justina did. Used in this way, the sign of the cross becomes a potent magical act that can repel hostile magic, drive off evil spirits, and purify our auras of chaotic thoughts and energies.

I'm aware that in using the term "aura" above, I may be stirring up a bit of controversy or confusion. In common use, the term "aura" refers to a notional sphere about three feet in diameter that surrounds the human form. The aura is at once an organ of perception and of projection—it is the "screen" on which your thoughts and emotions are projected, and the "window" through which you perceive spiritual realities. You'll sometimes find modern occultists claiming that it is a recent innovation, dreamed up perhaps by New Agers or Madame Blavatsky. But this is not so—you can find discussions of the aura in Proclus's work from the Fifth Century. Some people have the ability to see auras naturally, and others find that it develops over time; others can "sense" them in a more abstract way, rather than perceiving them with their physical senses.

With all that said, if the idea of auras makes you uncomfortable, you can read the sentence as though I'd said the sign of the cross can "purify our *minds* of chaotic thoughts and energies." It's just as true, and it works just as well.

The sign of the cross as banishing ritual

In the magical tradition, a ritual that works as I described above—that is to say, a protective ritual that can repel hostile magic, drive off evil spirits, and purify our auras of chaotic thoughts and energies—is known as a *banishing ritual*. In our work so far, we've been making the Sign of the Cross in a manner familiar to ordinary Catholic, Orthodox, and Anglican Christians. Of course, this works perfectly well, but there is more that can be done with the Sign of the Cross, and that's what I want to discuss now.

The banishing sign of the cross

The following ritual can be performed at any time, but it is best done before meditation or any act of magic or blessing.

Step 1. Imagine a brilliant point of light located at an infinite distance above your head. Know that this light is not God the Father, but is, rather, the closest that a human mind can come to comprehending the power of God the Father.

Step 2. Now, imagine a column of light descending from that remote point down through the cosmos, finally coming to rest at the crown of your head. Reach up with your right hand, and draw the light to your forehead. Vibrate* the words *"In Nomine Patris."*

*To "vibrate" means to chant in such a way that your voice creates a noticeable buzzing in your body, or in the space around you. If you're working with a specific part of the body, as in the point of light at the forehead, you should feel the buzzing there. Some people find this very easy to do; others struggle. If you're of the latter persuasion, just sing or chant the words, and imagine you can feel the vibration in your body.

Step 3. Draw your hand to your heart. As you do, bow your head, and imagine the column of light descending down, through the centerline of your body, and all the way into the heart of the Earth. Vibrate *Et Filii*.

Step 4. Draw your hand up and out to your left shoulder, and then your right shoulder. As you do so, visualize another line of white light rising up from the heart of the Earth, meeting the first at your heart, and then extending outward in either direction in infinite space. Vibrate *Et Spiritu Sancti*.

Step 5. Bring both of your hands together at your heart. Imagine a sphere of golden light at your heart. Vibrate the word *Amen*. As you do so, imagine that sphere expanding outward in every direction, until it surrounds you on all sides. Know that you are surrounded and protected by the Light divine.

Step 6. Say the Our Father, three Hail Marys, and Glory Be.

Step 7. After the prayers, make the Sign of the Cross again. This time, though, you can do so more quickly, closer to the way that people ordinarily do—though you should always pray with a reverent attitude. You will find, even if you rush through it, you will reconnect to the energy of the fuller ritual, so that any time you make the Sign of the Cross in daily life, it will have an added power and majesty.

From here on out, you should use the Banishing Sign of the Cross every time you perform the opening ritual.

Explanation and notes

In traditional Christian philosophy, the creative power of God is said to have three parts or movements. These movements are called abiding, proceeding, and returning. Abiding means remaining in stillness.

Proceeding is the work of God's creative activity going forth into the universe. Dionysius compares this with Light—not the visible light of our world, but the eternal light of the divine. This is the "light that shineth in the darkness, and the darkness could not grasp it." The third movement is returning, a word which can also be translated, very importantly, as "conversion." This is the process whereby all created things return to God, who is their source and origin.

At the same time, the Trinity is never truly divided, and all three persons are always present at the same time, in all three movements.

This is the special meaning of the "descent of the Holy Ghost" on the apostles at Pentecost. In one sense, the Spirit is said to "descend." At the same time, it is not so much that the Spirit goes anywhere as it is that the apostles themselves, through their continuous work of prayer, have elevated their own souls to the level at which the Spirit can be perceived—that's why the spirit descends on their heads, meaning the highest part of the souls. In another sense, the Spirit is the force which drives their prayer, leading them in the work of conversion.

Each of these movements is the special work of one of the three persons of the Holy Trinity. God the Father abides eternally in stillness. He speaks His Word, and His Son goes forth in the work of Creation. And all of Creation works ever to return to God, through the power of the Holy Spirit. At the same time, the Trinity is never separated; the Father, in another sense, goes forth and returns; the Son abides and returns; the Spirit abides and proceeds.

Spiritual practices can be compared to technology, but in an important sense they are not a technology. God's power or energy is not a force like electricity that we can manipulate at will. It isn't even a sentient animal like a horse or a dog that can be trained to follow commands. God's energy, with which we are working here, is God Himself manifest; it is alive and personal in a higher way than ourselves. You should see the Banishing Sign of the Cross not so much as a technique as a prayer. All prayer involves an element of thought. Most of the time, we think in words, as when a person silently prays "Our Father, who art in Heaven …" In this case, we are thinking in images—the light, the cross, the sphere. It is still a prayer.

As a prayer, it will always be answered. "Who among you, if your son asked for bread, would give him a stone?" God is a loving Father. But he must be approached with reverence and respect. Neither the Holy Trinity nor the saints and angels are subject to our command.

Finally, a note of caution. In the technical terms of magical philosophy, it is said that there are two great currents of magical power. [SOURCE See *Greer Druidry Handbook*] One descends from the Heavens; the other rises from the Earth. These are sometimes called the "Solar Current" and the "Telluric Current." When they are united, a third current, the "Lunar," is created.

These ideas are a bit outside the scope of this book, but they're worth mentioning for one reason. For most people, the simple banishing practice given here will work just fine. A small number of people, however, have difficulties working with the combination of currents. The way this typically manifests is through a sense of irritation and imbalance in the nervous system. If you experience this, try leaving out the visualization of the ascending light. Simply extend the light that descends from Heaven to the left and right, understanding it as the power of the Holy Spirit extending throughout creation.

If even that proves to be too much, simply perform the sign of the cross in the usual way.

PART THREE

SECOND WEEK OF ADVENT

CHAPTER TWELVE

Second Sunday in Advent

Today is the Second Sunday in Advent. Now the second week of our course begins. This week, we will encounter additional saints and celebrations and introduce several new techniques of Christian magic.

Readings for the Second Sunday in Advent

The Epistle for the Second Sunday is taken from Saint Paul's Letter to the Romans:

> For what things soever were written were written for our learning: that, through patience and the comfort of the scriptures, we might have hope. Now the God of patience and of comfort grant you to be of one mind, one towards another, according to Jesus Christ: That with one mind and with one mouth you may glorify God and the Father of Our Lord Jesus Christ. Wherefore, receive one another, as Christ also hath received you, unto the honour of God. For I say that Christ Jesus was minister of the circumcision for the truth of God, to confirm the promises made unto the fathers: But that the Gentiles are to glorify God for his mercy, as it is written: "Therefore will

I confess to thee, O Lord, among the Gentiles and will sing to thy name." And again he saith: "Rejoice ye Gentiles, with his people." And again: "Praise the Lord, all ye Gentiles: and magnify him, all ye people." And again, Isaias saith: "There shall be a root of Jesse; and he that shall rise up to rule the Gentiles, in him the Gentiles shall hope." Now the God of hope fill you with all joy and peace in believing: that you may abound in hope and in the power of the Holy Ghost.

And the Gospel reading comes from the first chapter of Matthew:

At that time, when John had heard in prison the works of Christ: sending two of his disciples he said to him: "Art thou he that art to come, or look we for another?" And Jesus making answer said to them:

> "Go and relate to John what you have heard and seen. The blind see, the lame walk, the lepers are cleansed, the deaf hear, the dead rise again, the poor have the Gospel preached to them. And blessed is he that shall not be scandalized in me."

And when they went their way, Jesus began to say to the multitudes concerning John:

> "What went you out into the desert to see? A reed shaken with the wind? But what went you out to see? A man clothed in soft garments? Behold they that are clothed in soft garments, are in the houses of kings. But what went you out to see? A prophet? Yea I tell you, and more than a prophet. For this is he of whom it is written: 'Behold I send my angel before my face, who shall prepare thy way before thee.'"

Meditation for the Second Sunday in Advent

Today in your meditation, consider the various themes drawn from the readings, and the symbolism of the second violet candle, which includes both peace and prophecy. Take note of the figure of John the

Baptist, described in the reading today by Our Lord Himself as the angel before the face of God. John's ministry comes before Jesus, and prepares the way for Jesus. How is this related to Saint Paul's discussion of the Gentiles in his letter? Please note: He says that "All things that were written were written for our learning." It was the ancient teaching of the Christian Church that this included the writings of the pagans, both in their myths and in their philosophy. In the ideas of Plato and Aristotle, they saw a glimmer of an understanding of the true nature of God. In the tales of the ancient heroes, like Odysseus struggling to find his way home, they saw an image of the Christian life. What other ideas, themes, sources of inspiration can you draw from these readings?

The Advent Wreath: Lighting the second candle

The second candle on the Advent Wreath is often called the Bethlehem Candle, and its theme is the theme of Peace.

Step 1. Begin in your usual way, with the sign of the cross by itself or with additional prayers.

Step 2. Read the following short verse from Psalm 46:

> God is our refuge and strength, a very present help in trouble.
>
> He maketh wars to cease unto the end of the earth; he breaketh the bow, and cutteth the spear in sunder; he burneth the chariot in the fire.
>
> Be still, and know that I am God: I will be exalted among the heathen, I will be exalted in the earth.
>
> The Lord of hosts is with us; the God of Jacob is our refuge.

Step 3. Pray: Oh God, as we light this candle, may it be for us a symbol of the Eternal Light of Thy Holy Spirit, and a sign of peace for we who wander in the darkness of the world. *Amen.*

Light the candle. As noted above, the theme of this candle is *peace*. At dinner, you can discuss the idea of peace with your family, what it means to them individually and for our larger world, and you may also take it as a theme for your meditations this week.

CHAPTER THIRTEEN

Saint Nicholas Day

December 6 is the Feast of Saint Nicholas. Again, please note: While I'm including this chapter on Saint Nicholas under the second week of Advent, some years his feast will fall during the first week of Advent! If that includes the current year, make sure not to neglect him during the first week.

Saint Nicholas has been venerated for quite a long time, and associated with the Christmas season and gifts for children since long before his current incarnation as Santa Claus. Let's talk about him, and the customs associated with his Feast Day.

The life of Saint Nicholas

The historical Saint Nicholas was a 4th-century Christian bishop, and the truth is that we know very little about his actual life. That isn't really the truth, though. If you start paying attention, you will find that the phrase "we know" is, like its cousin "is known," used constantly in modern life to talk about historical and scientific topics. But "we know" very often doesn't say anything about what "we" "know." It really means "This is what academics, college professors, and people who seek approval from academics and college professors think is true."

And so, the current consensus among college professors and their lackeys is that Nicholas was a bishop from the Greek town of Myra, who may or may not have attended the Council of Nicea in 325 AD. He also may or may not have punched the heretic Arius in the face when Arius continued to deny the full divinity of Jesus Christ.

Remember that in the Christian magical tradition, our perspective is that myth is more important than history. History happens once, and is over; myth never happens, but occurs again and again and again. Myth unfolds the reality of spiritual things at a level the human mind can grasp, and it describes the hidden patterns of meaning that lie just beneath the surface of our reality.

It can truly be said that myth exists at one of the levels of being that lies in between the world of Time that we experience and the Eternal Reality of God. Myths are outside of the Time that we know—and yet they are not purely eternal. They come into being at a particular moment in history. They change and evolve, their characters and the relationships between them shifting between geographic regions and eras of world history like the characters in a dream. And yet, they continually create the world we experience—in this case, by forming the behavior of human beings.

The saints are human beings who, through their spiritual practices, have ascended beyond the realms of Time and Matter to the higher worlds. As such, their biography, even when it is known, matters far, far less than the legends that gather around them.

Here are some of the legends of Saint Nicholas.

The real life of Saint Nicholas

Once there was a man who had lost his money through the trickery of the Devil. Now, this man had three daughters, and, with no dowry to provide for their marriages, he would be forced to sell them into prostitution. Hearing about the girls' plight, the local bishop, a man named Nicholas, resolved to help. But as he was a modest man, he was not willing to help openly, so that others would see. And so, under the cover of darkness, he snuck up to the family's house and tossed a purse full of gold through the window. Upon discovering it the next day, the girls' father was overjoyed. He immediately provided his oldest daughter with a dowry, and she was able to marry.

Upon hearing of the success of his first outing, Nicholas repeated the action a second time, and so the second daughter was able to marry. But the third time, the father resolved to stay awake and catch his secret patron in the act. Upon discovering that it was bishop Nicholas, the man fell to his knees and kissed the saint's feet. Nicholas admonished him to keep his charity a secret. Of course, the admonishment was ignored; otherwise, I would not be able to tell you about it.

Another time, three children were playing in the field, and forgot to keep an eye on the Sun. As there were no streetlights back then to tell the kids to get home before dark or to light their way back home, the children found themselves quite lost.

Fortunately, after a time, the children came across a butcher's shop on the road, still open and with its lights still on. Unfortunately, no one had told them that, in fairy tales, little children should by all means avoid lonely houses while lost in the woods, especially if they are lit up and welcoming, and especially if the nature of the house has anything at all to do with food. The butcher who kept the shop welcomed the children, fed them dinner, and provided them with a place to sleep for the night. Then he crept into their room, chopped them into pieces, and stored their salted bodies in a barrel.

Seven years later, the good bishop Nicholas happened to be wandering through the land. He came to the butcher shop and demanded to be let in. When he spied the barrel, in which the children's salted bodies were still aging, he made the Sign of the Cross over it and said, "Arise, oh children!" And the children got out of the barrel just as alive and well as the day they'd gotten into it.

Another time, Saint Nicholas heard about a tree which was possessed by a demon. Resolving to do something about it, he took an ax and cut the tree down. Now, ordinarily, such a thing is not sufficient to drive a demon off, but when the ax is swung by a saint, it does the job. Word of the saint's miracle spread throughout the region, so that several other villages suffering from demonic trees called upon Saint Nicholas, and he cut those down, too. And that's all that anyone really has to say about that.

Someone reading this might be upset that Nicholas cut down trees, and even more upset about the idea that a tree spirit could be evil. Let me tell you, as one who has experienced many tree spirits who were not evil, that there are some tree spirits out there who are very evil indeed, and others who simply hate human beings. If you happen to run into one of these evil trees, you can be sure that your Greenpeace membership will not impress them—but an invocation of Saint Nicholas just might!

Traditions of Saint Nicholas Day

In earlier times, many of Saint Nicholas's Christmas Eve duties were performed on the Eve of his Feast Day. It was only later, with the spread of Protestantism, that his cult was rolled into Christmas itself.

I have in my collection a fine old volume entitled *Christmas in Ritual and Tradition*, by Clement A. Miles. Writing over a century ago, Miles is quick to interpret everything interesting in Christianity as a "pagan survival." When you encounter claims like that, your best bet is to ignore them. Christianity is interesting all on its own, without having to be "secretly Pagan." That said, if you can overlook the book's one glaring flaw, it is a treasure trove of information on old customs. Here is what Miles has to say on the subject of Saint Nicholas Day:

> St. Nicholas's Eve is a time of festive stir in Holland and Belgium; the shops are full of pleasant little gifts: many-shaped biscuits, gilt gingerbreads, sometimes representing the saint, sugar images, toys, and other trifles. In many places, when evening comes on, people dress up as Saint Nicholas, with mitre and pastoral staff, inquire about the behavior of the children, and if it has been good, pronounce a benediction and promise them a reward next morning. Before they go to bed the children put out their shoes, with hay, straw, or a carrot in them for the saint's white horse or ass. When they wake in the morning, if they have been "good" the fodder is gone and sweet things or toys are in its place; if they have misbehaved themselves the provender is untouched and no gift but a rod is there.
>
> In various parts of Germany, Switzerland, and Austria Saint Nicholas is mimed by a man dressed up as a bishop. In Tyrol children pray to the saint on his Eve and leave out hay for his white horse and a glass of schnaps for his servant. And he comes in all the splendor of a church-image, a reverend gray-haired figure with flowing beard, gold-broidered cope, glittering mitre, and pastoral staff. Children who know their catechism are rewarded with sweet things out of the basket carried by his servant; those who

cannot answer are reproved, and Saint Nicholas points to a terrible form that stands behind him with a rod—the hideous Klaubauf, a shaggy monster with horns, black face, fiery eyes, long red tongue, and chains that clank as he moves.

In Lower Austria the saint is followed by a similar figure called Krampus or Grampus; in Styria this horrible attendant is named Bartel; all are no doubt related to such monsters as the Klapperbock. Their heathen origin is evident though it is difficult to trace their exact pedigree. Sometimes Saint Nicholas himself appears in a non-churchly form like Pelzmärte, with a bell, or with a sack of ashes which gains him the name of Aschenklas.

Notice the two features of Saint Nicholas: He only brings presents and candies to good children, leaving a rod for the bad ones; and he is accompanied by a goblin or monster who carries off the worst.

Never doubt, by the way, that Saint Nicholas actually does these things. He is no longer a man in a body, but a saint and a spirit. Unlike us sojourners here in the world of Matter and Time, spirits are not limited to a single body, and will happily make use of whatever body is provided for them. That very much includes the bodies of parents setting out treats for their children. Of course, the spirits often require that certain conditions are met before they'll descend into a human body—such as dressing up as a bishop, or donning a red coat and a red fur-trimmed cap.

Suggestions for practice

Most children in America and, I suspect, the rest of the Anglophone world, are unacquainted with Saint Nicholas Day. There are some exceptions. At a Catholic school near where I live, the children leave stockings outside the hall during their last period of the day, at which time they are filled with candy by the school's principal. And I know that North American converts to the Eastern Orthodox Church (often via the Antiochian archdiocese) often celebrate Saint Nicholas Day in the traditional manner. It probably isn't going to be possible to shift the entire tradition of Saint Nicholas back to his Feast Day, and it may not even be desirable to do so.

That said, we can still take steps toward reincorporating the old practices into our family Christmas celebrations. Children can leave their shoes out for Saint Nicholas the night before his Feast Day, or extra shoes left at home can be filled with treats while they are at school. This can be accompanied with a suitable prayer to Saint Nicholas, and an offering of food or drinks, according to taste.

Meditation for Saint Nicholas Day

Set up your prayer space or altar with a Saint Nicholas icon or prayer card, if you have one. Enter into meditation the usual way, opening with the sign of the cross and additional prayers. Then either concentrate on the icon or simply bring the saint to mind. If you like, you can visualize one of the stories from the life of Saint Nicholas. Then, imagine him coming to your home—perhaps as he used to in the olden days, on his white horse in his bishop's robe, rather than his new guise, in order to invoke the older meaning. Imagine him blessing the house and bringing gifts to all—but understand that the gift that he brings is not a material thing, but the spirit of giving freely of oneself.

And there is another gift he brings, too. Saint Nicholas is the patron, especially, of children, and is well-loved by them. Recall that Our Lord Himself teaches us that we will only enter into the Kingdom of Heaven if we do so as little children.

> Truly, I say to you, unless you turn and become like children,
> you will never enter the kingdom of heaven.

This is a deep, mystical teaching. To understand it, consider that children arrive on this Earth directly from the Presence of God, and the work of learning to function in ordinary human society is also the work of obscuring the light of Heaven from our eyes. Imagine that the gifts of Saint Nicholas are not merely given to children, but given to all of us, to awaken the part that is child-like in all of us. In the Taoist mystical traditions of China, this part of us is called the *yuan shen*, or "original spirit"—the part of our being that stands beyond all the conditioning of our culture and the experiences and traumas that shape our later habits of thought and mind.

(Please note: Many Christian churches teach that this isn't quite correct—they believe that the souls of babies are formed here on Earth, but the *idea* of every human being exists eternally in the Mind of God.

In practice, it amounts to much the same thing, and you are, as always, welcome to make up your own mind on these subjects.)

In meditation, imagine the experience of the Christmas season awakening us to our true being, and let this be the true meaning of the gifts of Saint Nicholas. If your St Nicholas icon or holy card has a specific prayer, you can close with that, or with your own prayer, such as:

> Oh God, we thank you for Saint Nicholas, and we pray that he may visit our homes this year, and awaken us to the joy of freely giving, and awaken, too, the original and child-like spirit within all of us, that we may become as the little children are, and enter into the Kingdom of Heaven. Good Saint Nicholas, patron of children, sailors, and the helpless, pray for us this day. *Amen.*

CHAPTER FOURTEEN

The Immaculate Conception

December 8 is the Feast Day of the Immaculate Conception, which is the conception of Mary. This feast always falls during Advent, and so is the first Marian feast of the year. And that is proper, as it is the feast of her conception, the moment her soul descended into the material world.

(Like Saint Nicholas's Day, the Feast of the Immaculate Conception will sometimes occur during the first week of Advent. As always, make sure to plan ahead so you know when to celebrate!)

Now, the Eastern Churches also celebrate the conception of the Virgin Mary on this day, but they don't use the term "Immaculate Conception." This term is specifically used in the Western Church to refer to Mary's having been conceived without Original Sin.

The idea of "Original Sin," meanwhile, has different meanings in the East and West, so let's talk about that for a moment.

Original Sin, East and West

In both Eastern and Western Christianity, the Original Sin is the sin committed by Adam and Eve when they disobeyed God's command and ate from the fruit of the Tree of Knowledge at the suggestion of the serpent. Everyone agrees on that, but here the two branches of Christendom part ways. In the East, the belief has always been that, at this moment, Sin and Death entered into the world. It's as if the transgression itself opened a kind of doorway. Sin and Death, now, aren't just actions or ideas—in a sense they're real beings, who did not have access to our world before our First Parents' transgression, but now do. The consequences of the Original Sin, then, are twofold: First, Sin is now in the world. We've become capable of it, we are always tempted by it, and at times all of us fall into it. The second consequence is quite simply that we die, since Death has been allowed into the world.

The West takes a rather harsher view of Original Sin. Following Saint Augustine, the teaching of the Western Church for many centuries is that every baby born into this world is, already, themselves, guilty of the sin of Adam and Eve. For this reason, infant Baptism is raised almost to the level of an emergency, as Baptism into the Christian Church is the only thing that can free us from the guilt of Original Sin. Lacking Baptism, a baby who dies prematurely is unable to enter into Heaven. Where it actually goes is a matter of debate; some, including Augustine, held the position that unbaptized babies descend immediately into Hell. Others believed that they departed to a middle realm called the Limbo of the Infants (*Limbus Infantium*) where they enjoyed every possible natural happiness, but were denied the Beatific Vision, which is the Presence of God itself.

Now, because the Christian West holds that every infant is conceived in sin and guilt, it was necessary to develop the doctrine of the Immaculate Conception. According to this view, God intervened in Mary's conception, removing the stain of Original Sin from her, in order to create an unblemished vessel for the incarnation of Jesus. Many of the Church Fathers write that she was restored at the moment of her conception to the Original Justice of Humanity before the Fall.

As the Christian East does not view Original Sin as a particular guilt possessed by every human infant, they did not require a special intervention by God to render Mary's conception sinless. They still celebrate her conception, though, as a miracle accomplished by God, who granted a child to saints Joachim and Anna, the parents of the Virgin Mary, in very old age.

Original Sin for Esoteric Christians

Readers who belong to one of the mainstream churches, or simply agree with their Mariology, are welcome to take any of the positions described above regarding the nature of Original Sin. My own perspective and that of many Esoteric Christians is different, though, and I'd like to take a minute to explore that here. (Orthodox believers may feel free to skip this section.)

According to the perspective of Esoteric Christianity, Original Sin has at least three different meanings:

1. **Past-Life Karma.** The Esoteric perspective is that none of us is here for the first time. Instead, the soul evolves through many cycles of incarnation and reincarnation before finally ascending to the eternal life that we call "Heaven." As the ancient Greek philosopher Plato wrote in the *Phaedo*, his great discussion of the soul and its existence after death, everything existing comes from its opposite; Death comes from Life, and the Living come into this world from the Dead. We aren't meant to remain here, but to transcend this world and return to the vision of God, from which our souls departed unnumbered eons ago. The fact that we are here, though, living in this world in which Sin is possible and Death comes to us all, shows us that we still have work to do. Only the sinless can enter into the Presence of God—and so the fact that we are reborn here shows that we still have the consequences of sins committed in prior lifetimes to work out. Borrowing a term from Eastern philosophy, this is often referred to as our karma or Past-Life Karma. This Past-Life Karma is one form of Original Sin.
2. **Collective Karma.** We human beings are not isolated individuals. We participate in society from the moment of our conception, when we share a body with our mother. We are dependent on and are part of our mothers, our families, our towns, regions, and nations. All of these collectives of human beings share a kind of collective mind and a collective soul, and every member of the collective participates in that soul. To one extent or another, we also all participate in the karma of the collectives into which we are born, for good or ill; the sins of our people, however defined, are, in a sense, ours. This manifests in our lives as the patterns of thought, reaction, emotion,

and behavior that are programmed into us by our families and our cultures, and which we manifest automatically. This is another sense of Original Sin: our birth into the Collective Karma of every group in which we take part. A major part of the work of spiritual development is the work of freeing the original spirit from the conditioning of its culture.

3. **Humanity's Karma.** There is an odd, possibly false, but fascinating idea that one finds scattered around 19th-century occult literature. This is the idea that the old legends about the Fall of Man that one finds in many ancient sources refer to a real event, many long millennia ago, in which human beings deliberately contacted the Demonic Plane. Demons, according to this way of thinking, are leftover souls from previous universes who refused the hard work of spiritual evolution. All that is left of those souls are these kinds of shells or husks, driven entirely by passion and with no capacity at all for reflective consciousness. Now they are incapable of growth or change. Like living addictions, they seek only to quench desires that are unquenchable, and to make any soul they encounter more like them. Because of this, they were walled off from the rest of the universe in some odd corner of the Astral Plane. And that's where human beings found them and released them, for purposes unknown. And so the rest of us get to spend the rest of our time as human beings dealing with an Astral Plane in which the ordinary human difficulties of cultural programming (the World) and unruly passions (the Flesh) are compounded by the presence of evil spirits (the Devil) who feed on and encourage our worst impulses.

The Immaculate Conception for Esoteric Christians

If Mary was conceived without Original Sin, she was conceived without being subject to any of the three forms of Original Sin described above. What would that mean?

First, she had worked out all of her individual karma through many lifetimes of spiritual practice. When she returned to material incarnation, it was as a being free from any debts from previous lifetimes.

Second, because she was such an advanced soul, she never allowed herself to be subject to cultural conditioning. Now, every source shows us that she did willingly and gladly participated in her culture. But she did so as a free spirit—the type of person who can choose her own thoughts and actions, rather than having them chosen for her.

Third, she was not subject to the influence of malevolent spirits. How could that be? In old China, when a mountain was known to be infested with demons, they would find a Taoist adept and send him to the mountain. There he would find a cave, sit, and meditate. It was said that a great meditator could calm every demon and unquiet ghost within a thousand miles. It's likely that, in life, Mary would have been just such an adept, spreading peace through the whole world by her mere presence.

Only such a being could become the vessel that could contain the Living God, the channel for all the grace poured out by God into the universe. Today, we celebrate her entrance into the world of matter and her great role in the history of salvation.

Prayer and meditation

Today, take the Immaculate Conception itself as the theme for your meditation—either the mainstream or orthodox version, or the esoteric interpretations that I provide.

It's worth noting, too, that Our Lady of the Immaculate Conception is the patron saint of the United States of America. If you happen to have any concerns about the current direction or ultimate fate of this country, today is a good time to make that known in prayer.

O Mary, conceived without sin, pray for us who have recourse to thee.

CHAPTER FIFTEEN

Foundations of Christian Magic: Almsgiving and Offerings

Take heed that ye do not your alms before men, to be seen of them: otherwise ye have no reward of your Father which is in heaven.

Therefore when thou doest thine alms, do not sound a trumpet before thee, as the hypocrites do in the synagogues and in the streets, that they may have glory of men. Verily I say unto you, They have their reward.

But when thou doest alms, let not thy left hand know what thy right hand doeth:

> That thine alms may be in secret: and thy Father which seeth in secret himself shall reward thee openly.

We already discussed charity and almsgiving way back at the beginning of this section, in Chapter 1. Now that we have some grounding in the practice of prayer and meditation, I'd like to take some time to explore this concept more fully.

In the Christian tradition, almsgiving isn't optional; in the words of the Gospel quoted above, Jesus doesn't say "If you give alms, do so in secret"; he says when you give alms, do so in secret.

The practice of giving alms has a number of important effects on the soul and on spiritual development. Let's take a moment to review the anatomy of the soul, and then talk about why we give alms, and how almsgiving can be used strategically to bring about changes we desire in our world and our lives.

Psychic anatomy

In the old tradition inherited by the Christian fathers from the Platonists before them, the soul is understood to consist of three parts. In Greek, these are called *Nous*, *Thymos*, and *Epithymia*. Now, the *Nous* refers to our minds; it includes our reason and our opinions, but at its highest it is our capacity to perceive spiritual reality. As we have already seen, the *Nous* is the same as what we're calling the Intellect, and at its highest, it is able to perceive the Intellectual Plane. *Thymos* is hard to translate—it is often rendered "spirit," but this is used in the sense that we would talk about "a spirited horse," or about someone being "in good spirits," rather than "spirit" as in "eternal soul." Its best translation in English is probably "heart," in the sense that this term is used in sports. "It's the team with the most heart that will win the match." *Epithymia*, meanwhile, is appetite, and includes all of the appetites, drives, and passions of our bodies.

Each of these components of the soul has its proper mode of functioning, and each has its particular disorder. The appetite wants to rebel and become our master, driving us to indulge every craving for food or drugs or sex or TikTok it can come up with. The *Nous* wants to cloud over and forget its true nature, becoming a mere repeater of worldly opinion instead of a seer of heavenly truth. And the *Thymos*? Well, the *Thymos* just wants to fight.

The work of spiritual advancement is called *repentance* in the Gospels. This is a translation of the Greek word metanoia, which literally means "to change the *Nous*." Through this work of metanoia, we change every aspect of our souls, re-orienting them away from the created world and toward eternal things. For each component of the soul, there is a particular spiritual discipline given to us as a sort of medicine, to heal and restore it to its proper functioning. For the *Nous*, we are given prayer; for the *Epithymia*, fasting; and for the *thymos*, almsgiving.

Fridays in Advent

Advent, as we have seen, is a penitential season. This means that we make use of it to double-down on our works of repentance, to purify our souls and prepare them for the coming of Our Lord at Christmas—which is, as we've seen, itself a preparation for the coming of the Lord to us at our own deaths, and to the whole world at the End of Time.

And so we fast from food and other material goods such as technology to discipline our appetites; we re-commit ourselves to prayer, to open the eye of our souls to the vision of God—

And we give, to purify our hearts and participate in the nature of God, who by His very nature gives constantly to all that exists.

Fridays are particularly good days for giving, for the following reasons:

1. Friday is a penitential day. Friday is the traditional day for fasting in the Catholic Church; until the 1960s, Catholics were expected to abstain from meat on this day throughout the year and to keep the full fast during penitential seasons.
2. Friday is associated with the Sacred Heart of Jesus. Each day of the week has its traditional spiritual association. Saturdays are devoted to the Virgin Mary; Sundays to the Holy Trinity and the Resurrection of Christ; Mondays to the Holy Ghost and the Souls in Purgatory; Tuesday to the Holy Angels; Wednesday to Saint Joseph; Thursday, to the Blessed Sacrament. And Friday? Friday is particularly dedicated to the Sacred Heart of Jesus. By giving alms on this day, we imitate Jesus, who freely gave of himself, first, to bring the world into being; second, at Calvary, to redeem us; third, at all times, to sustain our ongoing existence and that of the whole world and everything in it. Remember that, in the magical way of looking at things, two things never resemble each other by "accident" or "coincidence." To imitate Christ is to participate in the very being of Christ.
3. Friday is the Day of Venus. In the astrological tradition, every day is linked to one of the seven classical planets. Friday—in Latin, "Dies Veneris," "Day of Venus"—is associated with Venus, the planet of Love and Beauty. In Christian Astrology, the planets are visible signs given by God to reveal something about His nature to us; each planet is governed by an angel, and is associated with a particular

Christian virtue. The angel of Venus is named Hanael or Anael, and its particular virtue is Charity.

The magical uses of almsgiving

Alms can, and should, be given at any time, to anyone, for any reason, with the only limit being that set by morality. It's a good habit to give for no reason at all, at no particular time—leave the occasional 50% tip; give a homeless person an unusually large bill; find a charity dedicated to a cause you rarely think about, and given them a hundred dollars. In a real sense, this is the highest form of charity, and we ought to engage in it regularly.

That said, there are also good reasons to give alms at certain times, and to certain people and organizations. And we can also use other methods to increase the power of our offerings.

1. **Timing.** Spiritual timing occurs in a couple of different forms. We have the liturgical calendar, including Feast Days and seasons of fasting. As we have seen above, we have the traditional dedication of particular days and months to particular saints and spiritual forces. And we have the astrological cycle mentioned above. All of these days are like power points on the Wheel of the Year; appropriate activities, done at these times, are strengthened and enhanced by the energy of the time.
2. **Saints and Offerings.** We can increase the power of our offerings by making them in the name of a particular saint or angel. We usually do this in order to bring about specific purposes, related to the saint or angel's patronage. For example, Saint Joseph is the patron of workers. We can make offerings to a Church or charity named for him when we ourselves are looking for a job. We can also make the offering in his name to something under his patronage, like a job training program, even if it isn't named for him. Similarly, Saint Raphael the Archangel is the patron of healers; Saint Francis is the patron of animals and ecology; Saint Therese is an unofficial patron of alcoholics; Saint Michael watches over police, soldiers, and firefighters; and so on.
3. **Manifestation.** It is a spiritual truism that whatever we put out into the world also manifests in our own lives. It's not, as people sometimes say, that it "returns" to us—because that implies that it goes

somewhere else and then comes back. It is, rather, the case that whatever energy we participate in, for good or ill, manifests within us at that exact moment. If we bless another person, we are ourselves blessed; if we forgive, we are forgiven; if we give, we receive what we have given. Thus, if there is a change that you want to bring about in your life, giving to others will allow it to come to you as well. This is one reason why we should give what we can to our churches or spiritual leaders—we want the grace and the teaching that they have to offer to manifest in our lives, and so we participate in sustaining them.

Time for giving

Today, spend some time in prayer and meditation, and then make a donation to an organization, charity, or individual suitable to you. You can make a ritual out of this, first following the guide to prayer and meditation that I've posted here before, and then donating in the name of or for the cause of a suitable saint, or you can simply send a few dollars to a Church or a nonprofit through their website. Always add a blessing, and always give without expectation of reward—the reward has already manifested in your life by the very act of giving! "Thy Father which seest in secret shall reward thee openly."

PART FOUR

THIRD WEEK OF ADVENT

CHAPTER SIXTEEN

Third Sunday in Advent (Guadete Sunday)

Gaudete in Domino semper

Today is the third Sunday in Advent, called "Gaudete Sunday." Gaudete is a Latin word, meaning "Rejoice"; the Introit for the day begins "Gaudete in domino semper," or "Rejoice in the Lord always."

On Gaudete Sunday, the third, rose-colored candle on the Advent Wreath is lit; at the Mass, the priest may wear rose-colored vestments. Remember that the violet of the other three candles signifies darkness, sorrow, and repentance. Today, the rose candle is lit, as this is also a season of joy.

Readings for Gaudete Sunday

The Epistle for Gaudete Sunday is taken from Saint Paul's letter to the Philippians. In keeping with the theme of the day, it reminds us of the constant Presence of God:

> Brethren: Rejoice in the Lord always; again I say, rejoice. Let your moderation be known to all men. The Lord is near. Have no anxiety, but in every prayer and supplication with thanksgiving let your petitions be made known to God. And may the peace of God which

surpasses all understanding guard your hearts and your minds in Christ Jesus, Our Lord.

And the Gospel reading comes from the first chapter of John. In this selection, John the Baptist, whom we will meet again soon in our journey through the Christmas season, is being questioned about his identity:

> At that time, when the Jews sent from Jerusalem priests and Levites to him, to ask him: "Who art thou?" And he confessed and did not deny: and he confessed: "I am not the Christ." And they asked him: "What then? Art thou Elias?" And he said: "I am not." "Art thou the prophet?" And he answered: "No." They said therefore unto him: "Who art thou, that we may give an answer to them that sent us? What sayest thou of thyself?" He said: "I am the voice of one crying in the wilderness, make straight the way of the Lord, as said the prophet Isaias." And they that were sent were of the Pharisees. And they asked him and said to him: "Why then dost thou baptize, if thou be not Christ, nor Elias, nor the prophet?" John answered them, saying: "I baptize with water: but there hath stood one in the midst of you, whom you know not. The same is he that shall come after me, who is preferred before me: the latchet of whose shoe I am not worthy to loose." These things were done in Bethania, beyond the Jordan, where John was baptizing.

Meditation for Gaudete Sunday

Today in your meditation, consider the various themes drawn from the readings, and the symbolism of the rose candle. In John the Baptist, we see that the current of initiatic power that will be fully manifested in the person of Jesus has persisted all through the times of darkness before his coming. In the letter of Saint Paul, as in the introit to Mass, we are instructed to rejoice always. In the joyous rose candle, set amidst the penitential purple, we are shown the possibility of dwelling in the spiritual world—keeping the eye of our souls singular and fixed on the True Light, even as we sojourn in the darkness of the material world.

Happy Gaudete Sunday!

THIRD SUNDAY IN ADVENT (GUADETE SUNDAY)

The Advent Wreath: Lighting the third candle

As you might expect, the theme of the third candle is Joy.

Ritual for lighting the third candle

Step 1. Begin in your usual way, with the sign of the cross by itself or with additional prayers.

Step 2. Read the following short verse from the Psalm 5:

> But let all those that put their trust in thee rejoice: let them ever shout for joy, because thou defendest them: let them also that love thy name be joyful in thee.

Step 3. Pray:

> Oh God, as we light this candle, may it be for us a symbol of the Eternal Light of Thy Holy Spirit, and a sign of joy for we who wander in the darkness of the lower world. *Amen.*

Light the candle.

CHAPTER SEVENTEEN

Saint Lucy's Day

Today is Saint Lucy's Day, a feast little kept in America, even among Catholics. Historically, it was celebrated throughout much of the Old World. Let's talk about Saint Lucy, and some of the traditional customs of her Feast Day, and then discuss how we might engage with her in our magical practice.

The life of Saint Lucy

Saint Lucy lived in Syracuse during the time of the Emperor Diocletian's persecution of the Christians. A Christian herself, she dedicated her virginity to the Church. Unfortunately, when she was young her father died, and her mother decided to find a husband for her; she therefore had her betrothed to a wealthy young man from a Pagan family. Before we condemn her mother, it's worth remembering those times, "property" was still a kind of religious institution, held by males in a particular family line; it consisted of tending a family sacred fire, and making offerings to the spirits of the family's ancestors. Lacking a male head of household, women were more or less out of luck.

Now, it happened that Lucy's mother had a bleeding condition, which had troubled her for quite some time. Either Lucy's mother or

Lucy herself—stories vary—made a pilgrimage to the shrine of Saint Agatha; in either case, Saint Agatha visited Lucy in a dream and told her that her mother's faith would heal her. Lucy's mother was promptly healed, and agreed to give away all of her considerable wealth, even as Jesus enjoins his followers in the Gospels.

Word of this reached Lucy's fiancée, who was less than pleased, as the wealth that Lucy's mother gave away had necessarily to include Lucy's dowry. He ratted the girl out to Paschasius, the governor of Syracuse, who had her arrested.

While imprisoned, Lucy foretold the death of Paschasius and the end of Diocletian's persecutions. Enraged, the governor had her eyes torn out, and sentenced her to be defiled in a brothel. When her guards attempted to take her to the brothel, however, they found they were unable to move her. Resolving to burn her instead, they heaped wood about her, but it refused to light. Finally, one of the guards thrust his sword through her throat, and it seems that did the trick. One very often finds these two- or three-part deaths in the lives of the saints, and I suspect a close examination of them in meditation would be very fruitful. At her funeral, it was discovered that her eyes had been miraculously restored; of course, her prophecies later came true, as Paschasius met his end, and so did the purges of Diocletian.

Traditional celebrations

Over the long centuries of Christendom, many different customs sprang up around Saint Lucy's Day. In Sweden, it was called "Little Yule" and marked the beginning of the Christmas festival. There, it was the custom for a girl to dress in a white robe with a red sash, wear a crown in which nine lit candles were placed, and wake everyone up early with coffee and a special song. The family then had a fine breakfast together in a room lit with candles, and even the household animals were given special treats.

In Sicily, Saint Lucy's Day is celebrated with torchlit processions and bonfires. We can see that one of the main themes of her celebration is the presence of light. Lucy's name is a cognate of the Latin *lux*, meaning light, and it's been speculated that this is the reason for the focus on light during her festival. I would suggest, rather, that two things never resemble one another by "coincidence," but only because they participate in a common source. Our forebears, wiser than we, knew this, and so knew that God would not have given Lucy a name to remind us of Light for no good reason.

Other Saint Lucy's Day customs relate to divination in particular. In Denmark, girls traditionally made use of Saint Lucy's Day to discover the names of their future husbands. In Austria, it was a time to bless the house with incense to ward off witchcraft. In Christmas in Ritual and Tradition, our old friend Miles also describes a very interesting Saint Lucy's Day tradition from the same region:

At midnight, the girls practice a strange ceremony: they go to a willow-bordered brook, cut the bark of a tree partly away, without detaching it, make with a knife a cross on the inner side of the cut bark, moisten it with water, and carefully close up the opening. On New Year's Day, the cutting is opened, and the future is augured from the markings found. The lads, on the other hand, look out at midnight for a mysterious light, the Luzieschein, the forms of which indicate coming events.

In North America, immigrant communities from Sweden, Sicily, and elsewhere have preserved versions of the Saint Lucy's Day custom in certain parts of the country, particularly the Midwest. Unlike the Christmas Tree, however, these traditions haven't spread beyond those communities into the country as a whole, and now they are in danger of dying out altogether as the patchwork of European cultures that marked the United States in the 19th and 20th centuries continues to fade into the crumbling postindustrial gray of the 21st. The question before us is whether we can revive the older traditions, or, what would in my view be much better, rework them into something suitable for our own time. And, I would add, for my countrymen, rework them into something uniquely American, rather than European.

Suggestions for practice

We can see from the foregoing that there are two major themes associated with Saint Lucy's Day. These are the celebration of light in the darkness of winter, which is, of course, the major theme of the Christmas season as a whole, and the practice of divination. Of course, these are not at all unrelated. Rather than vain or anxious fortune-telling, the true purpose of divination is to open our inner eye to the Hidden Light of the spiritual world, in which Time does not run the way it does here. (As always, readers uncomfortable with divination are advised to ignore these parts.)

In meditation, today, we can contemplate the life of Saint Lucy, asking for the courage to face death as she did, and the wisdom to know hidden things, as she did. We can also use this day as an opportunity for divination. Sitting at our altars, with a candle lit, we might imagine that a new light begins to enter the world today, bringing with it the first hint of the year to come. Taking a moment to be aware of the light, we might then make our divinations, asking what we might need to know about the year ahead of us.

Now, divination can come in many different forms. For many readers, this will be a good time to make use of tarot cards, horary astrology, or the oracle of Geomancy. For others, it will be enough to simply pray to God and to Saint Lucy for wisdom and a clear vision. After doing this, sit in silence for a time, and be aware of whatever thoughts come to mind. Write these down; some may prove to be true visions of the future.

One very traditional method of Christian divination is called *bibliomancy*. This consists of asking a question and opening a suitable book to a random page. Of course, the best book to use for this practice is none other than the Bible itself. This sort of divination has a very long history in America. In *Albion's Seed*, the brilliant history of the deep structure of American culture by David Hackett Fischer, the author describes a Puritan son in the 1600s attempting to convince his parents to emigrate to America. The boy took down a Bible, opened it to a random page, and read "Come out from among them, touch no unclean thing, and I will be your God and you shall be my people" The entire family promptly made their way to New England! If you don't have a regular practice of divination, you might consider taking down a Bible, asking for a particular verse to guide you in the year to come, and opening it at random.

Now, it needs to be said that divination can be, and often is, misused; this is one of the reasons that many spiritual traditions warn against it. Its proper use is best described in the Book of Acts, Chapter 1, Verses 23–26. In this scene, the apostles are trying to figure out who should replace Judas, the traitor:

> And they proposed two: Joseph called Barsabas, who was surnamed Justus, and Matthias. And they prayed and said, "You, O Lord, who know the hearts of all, show which of these two You have chosen to take part in this ministry and apostleship from which Judas by transgression fell, that he might go to his own place." And they cast their lots, and the lot fell on Matthias. And he was numbered with the 11 apostles.

CHAPTER EIGHTEEN

Ember Days

Of all of the neglected traditions of Christendom, the Ember Days are among those most worthy of a revival. The Ember Days are a sequence of four three-day fasts, falling roughly around the beginning of each of the four seasons. Today marks the start of the Winter Embertide. Fasting is practiced on Wednesday, Friday and Saturday of this week.

It's very interesting to look at the reasons traditionally given for the Ember Fast. Here is a selection from Jacobo de Voragine's discussion of the custom in the 13th century. I'm going to quote it at length, and it's worth your time to read. I'm aware, though, that some people find medieval writing difficult to slog through; if that includes you, I'll see you on the next page!

> For the first time, which is in March, is hot and moist. The second, in summer, is hot and dry. The third, in harvest, is cold and dry. The fourth in winter is cold and moist. Then let us fast in March which is printemps for to repress the heat of the flesh boiling, and to quench luxury or to temper it. In summer we ought to fast to the end that we chastise the burning and ardor of avarice. In harvest

for to repress the drought of pride, and in winter for to chastise the coldness of untruth and of malice.

The second reason why we fast four times; for these fastings here begin in March in the first week of the Lent, to the end that vices wax dry in us, for they may not all be quenched; or because that we cast them away, and the boughs and herbs of virtues may grow in us. And in summer also, in the Whitsun week, for then cometh the Holy Ghost, and therefore we ought to be fervent and esprized in the love of the Holy Ghost. They be fasted also in September tofore Michaelmas, and these be the third fastings, because that in this time the fruits be gathered and we should render to God the fruits of good works. In December they be also, and they be the fourth fastings, and in this time the herbs die, and we ought to be mortified to the world.

The third reason is for to ensue the Jews. For the Jews fasted four times in the year, that is to wit, tofore Easter, tofore Whitsunside, tofore the setting of the tabernacle in the temple in September, and tofore the dedication of the temple in December.

The fourth reason is because the man is composed of four elements touching the body, and of three virtues or powers in his soul: that is to wit, the understanding, the will, and the mind. To this then that this fasting may attemper in us four times in the year, at each time we fast three days, to the end that the number of four may be reported to the body, and the number of three to the soul. These be the reasons of Master Beleth.

The fifth reason, as saith John Damascenus: in March and in printemps the blood groweth and augmenteth, and in summer choler, in September melancholy, and in winter phlegm. Then we fast in March for to attemper and depress the blood of concupiscence disordinate, for sanguine of his nature is full of fleshly concupiscence. In summer we fast because that coler should be lessened and refrained, of which cometh wrath. And then is he full naturally of ire. In harvest we fast for to refrain from melancholy. The melancholious man naturally is cold, covetous and heavy. In winter, we fast for to daunt and to make feeble the phlegm of lightness and forgetting, for such is he that is phlegmatic.

The sixth reason is for the printemps [Spring] is likened to the air, the summer to fire, harvest to the earth, and the winter to water.

Then we fast in March to the end that the air of pride be attempered to us. In summer the fire of concupiscence and of avarice. In September the earth of coldness and of the darkness of ignorance. In winter the water of lightness and inconstancy.

The seventh reason is because that March is reported to infancy, summer to youth, September to steadfast age and virtuous, and winter to anciency or old age. We fast then in March that we may be in the infancy of innocency. In summer for to be young by virtue and constancy. In harvest that we may be ripe by attemperance. In winter that we may be ancient and old by prudence and honest life, or at least that we may be satisfied to God of that which in these four seasons we have offended him.

The eighth reason is of Master William of Auxerre. We fast, saith he, in these four times of the year to the end that we make amends for all that we have failed in all these four times, and they be done in three days each time, to the end that we satisfy in one day that which we have failed in a month; and that which is the fourth day, that is Wednesday, is the day in which Our Lord was betrayed of Judas; and the Friday because Our Lord was crucified; and the Saturday because he lay in the sepulchre, and the apostles were sore of heart and in great sorrow.

Here we see that the medieval mind explicitly linked together high theology and the liturgical cycle with the cycles of the natural world and an energetic approach to healing and medicine. If you've ever studied Traditional Chinese Medicine you may be familiar with the concepts of the qi nodes and of *jia qi*. The latter literally means "energy of the calendar," and refers to the cycles of yin and yang and the five elements of Chinese philosophy throughout the year. The system of qi nodes is a way of tracking the calendar energy. There are 24 qi nodes set along the Wheel of the Year, including the solstices, equinoxes, and what we call the cross-quarter days. In TCM theory, there are specific practices, ranging from dietary medicines to personal habits to meditation and qigong which one undertakes in order to promote health by aligning oneself correctly with the cyclic energy of the seasons. In the Ember Days, we see that the same set of ideas was present at one time in the Western world—suitable to Western philosophy, religion and culture.

Winter Ember Days: The element of Earth

You'll notice that Bishop Voragine specifically links Winter to the Water element, which is understood as coldness and moisture. Elemental attributions are not arbitrary, but neither are they fixed; different people in different times and places have seen the elements somewhat differently. These days, we're more likely to describe Winter as relating to the element of Earth, with Water reserved for the Fall, when rains come and fruits (containing the watery life of the plant) are harvested. It's less about discovering truths fixed in stone and more about finding a method that works. As the element assigned to Winter, the cold, dry element of Earth works as well as Water or better; Air would work poorly; Fire would not work at all.

In esoteric thought, each of the elements is linked to one of the four archangels, and that archangel can be invoked as the governor of the element in question. The elemental archangels are as follows:

- Earth – Uriel
- Air – Raphael
- Fire – Michael
- Water – Gabriel

Now, the four elements, it must be remembered, are not four elementary particles. There are four phases of existence into which all things can be divided. In addition to its association with Winter, Earth includes all of the following:

Midnight in times; old age in a lifetime; the body in man; soil and stone in nature; the root in plants, and mosses and other plants that creep along the ground; among herbs, all those cold and moist by temperament; among animals, those that live in the soil; among professions, those related to the Earth, including farmers and miners, and all those who work with their hands, and also beggars; in society, it is the physical environment, both natural and man-made; among planets, it is Saturn (others say Venus); among numbers, the number 4 and all its permutations; among shapes, the cube.

The Ember Fast

This week, extend whatever fasting commitment you've made to Wednesday, Friday, and Saturday. In addition, make at least one additional effort toward lightening your impact on the Earth—turning the heat down a couple of degrees might be particularly appropriate, as it will allow you to more fully connect with the cold, which is Earth. On at least one of these days, spend some additional time in nature. Allow yourself to be aware of the Earth element as it manifests in the stones and the soil and the physical structure of the world in general, as well as those creatures that are specifically governed by it. You might also consider donating to an Earth-oriented charity, such as an organization dedicated to helping farmers, miners, the elderly or the very poor.

Prayer and meditation

At least once, and preferably during all three days, practice the following meditation:

Step 1. Make the Sign of the Cross.

Step 2. Say the Our Father, three Hail Marys, and Glory Be.

Step 3. Perform the asperges with holy water and the censing with incense, using the prayers previously given. In a pinch, you can use ordinary water into which a little bit of salt has been added. Before using it, make the sign of the cross over it and ask God for his blessing.

Step 4. Pray the Prayer of the Holy Spirit:

> Come, Holy Spirit, fill the hearts of Thy faithful and enkindle in them the fire of Thy love.
>
> Send forth Thy Spirit and they shall be created, and Thou shalt renew the face of the earth.
>
> Let us pray.
>
> O God, Who didst instruct the hearts of the faithful by the light of the Holy Spirit, grant us in the same Spirit to be truly wise, and ever to rejoice in His consolation, through Christ, Our Lord. Amen.

Step 5. Kneeling or seated, take a few moments to relax your body and clear your mind with rhythmic breathing. Then call to mind the Earth element and the Winter season, and everything pertaining to them. Offer a prayer, such as the following:

> Oh God, I thank thee for all the gifts of the element of Earth. For solidity and stability, the long nights and the winter snows, and all the gifts of the physical world. And I pray that thou wilt send thy holy archangel Uriel, who governs the element Earth, to be with us at this time. Holy Saint Uriel, archangel who governs the element

of Earth, grant that the gifts and virtues of Earth, industriousness, temperance, and tranquility of spirit may be manifest in our lives. And grant, too, that the unbalanced manifestations of Earth, including avarice, sloth and despondency, may be kept far from us. Through Jesus Christ Our Lord, Amen.

Step 6. Take a moment to visualize the gifts and virtues of Earth manifesting in your life. Then close your meditation with more rhythmic breathing.

Step 7. If you like, you can repeat the asperges and the censing.

Step 8. Close with a suitable prayer or prayers, followed by the sign of the cross. The Fatima Prayer is a good option:

> O my Jesus, forgive us our sins, save us from the fires of hell. Lead all souls to Heaven, especially those in most need of thy mercy. Amen.

CHAPTER NINETEEN

Foundations of Christian Magic: Forgiveness

It may surprise you to hear "forgiveness" described as a type of magic. In fact, it is very powerful magic indeed. Remember the teaching of our magical philosophy. All of our minds are connected on the Astral Plane. When we hold onto anger, hatred, jealousy, or resentment, both we ourselves and the target of our negative emotions are feel the effects. Moreover, whenever we feel these things toward another person, it is very likely that they are feeling the same thing toward us. Hatred and anger can "bounce" back and forth between two people in this way. It is as though the two souls were linked by an invisible but toxic chord, causing harm to both.

These sorts of toxic chords are the basis for what is called the "evil eye" in many traditions: That is, the idea that someone thinking negative thoughts about you or looking at you with jealousy effectively puts a curse on you.

The Scriptures themselves teach this in many different places. In Ecclesiastes, we read:

> Curse not the king, no not in thy thought; and curse not the rich in thy bedchamber: for a bird of the air shall carry the voice, and that which hath wings shall tell the matter.

Now, King Solomon was smarter than you and me, and I'm sure you know that he wasn't talking about actual birds carrying your thoughts through the actual air. No—he meant that our thoughts themselves affect their subjects, especially when they are charged by strong emotion.

Moreover, Our Lord Himself teaches us this same principle in the Gospel of Matthew:

> You have heard that it was said, "You shall not commit adultery." But I say to you that every one who looks at a woman lustfully has already committed adultery with her in his heart.

And again in the Gospel of John:

> Any one who hates his brother is a murderer, and you know that no murderer has eternal life abiding in him.

Notice what he is saying. It isn't "Don't hate people or look at women with lust, because if you do you're going to get into big trouble." No: He is teaching us that when we hate, we are already guilty of murder; when we look at someone with inappropriate lust, we are already guilty of adultery. Now, murder and adultery both require two parties: a murderer and a victim or an adulterer and a co-adulterer. And so we see that the true teaching is precisely what we have been saying here. Our minds have never been limited to our own heads. What we think and feel toward other people affects them, and affects us.

When we sincerely forgive, we free ourselves from the web of toxicity that binds us to others. Moreover, rather than simply "cutting the chords," we can set up a new chord through which the higher energies of love and blessing can flow. Remember that, in magic, whatever we do to someone else affects us at just the same time, in just the same way.

A ritual of forgiveness

Preparation. Set up your working space with an altar, candle, crucifix, and other implements. In addition to these things, you are going to need at least one person you want to forgive. Of course, you may be one of those rare people who's already forgiven everyone in their life for everything they've ever done to hurt you. If that's the case, then you can broaden your scope to include groups, institutions, places, or even entire countries. (If nothing comes to mind, think about contemporary politics. I'm sure that you'll find at least one person or group whom you just can't stop being angry at.)

Step 1. Perform the opening ceremony, including the Banishing Sign of the Cross, if you are making use of it.

Please note: This is one ritual that can be performed any time, any place you can find a few minutes to be left alone. You can do the forgiveness ritual in a church, on a park bench, or while riding on a bus. Or even while pretending to nap at a coffee shop.

Step 2. Close your eyes. Say the Lord's Prayer silently to yourself, focusing on the words "forgive us our trespasses, as we forgive those who trespass against us."

Step 3. Bring to mind the person or group you wish to forgive. Try to imagine the situation entirely from the other person's perspective. Imagine what might have led them to do the things they did or to say the things they say. Imagine yourself doing and saying these things. Imagine yourself as the other person (or group, etc.) must see you.

Step 4. Once you feel that you have totally entered into the other party's perspective, and once you are sure you can say this and mean it, silently say: "I understand that you can only be who you are. I forgive you. I forgive you. I forgive you. I am sorry for everything that I did to hurt you, and I hope that you will forgive me."

Step 5. Come out of meditation in the usual way, closing with a suitable prayer and the sign of the cross.

It is important that you place no expectations on this practice. The other person may or may not forgive you; their behavior toward you may or may not change. The point is that you have forgiven them. As the Prayer of Saint Francis reminds us, "It is by forgiving that we are forgiven."

PART FIVE

FOURTH WEEK OF ADVENT

PART TWO

CHAPTER TWENTY

Fourth Sunday in Advent

Welcome to the Fourth Sunday in Advent! I hope that this course has served you well up to this point, and that you've continued the practices of prayer and meditation, fasting, and almsgiving, as well as incorporating the magical practices presented.

The Epistle for the Fourth Sunday is taken from Saint Paul's letter to the Corinthians:

> Brethren: Let a man so account of us as of the ministers of Christ and the dispensers of the mysteries of God. Here now, it is required among the dispensers that a man be found faithful. But to me it is a very small thing to be judged by you or by man's day. But neither do I judge my own self. For I am not conscious to myself of anything. Yet am I not hereby justified: but he that judgeth me is the Lord. Therefore, judge not before the time: until the Lord come, who both will bring to light the hidden things of darkness and will make manifest the counsels of the hearts. And then shall every man have praise from God.

And the Gospel reading comes from the Gospel of Luke:

> Now in the fifteenth year of the reign of Tiberius Caesar, Pontius Pilate being governor of Judea, and Herod being tetrarch of Galilee, and Philip his brother tetrarch of Iturea and the country of Trachonitis, and Lysanias tetrarch of Abilina: Under the high priests Anna and Caiphas: the word of the Lord was made unto John, the son of Zachary, in the desert. And he came into all the country about the Jordan, preaching the Baptism of penance for the remission of sins. As it was written in the book of the sayings of Isaias the prophet: "A voice of one crying in the wilderness: Prepare ye the way of the Lord, make straight his paths. Every valley shall be filled and every mountain and hill shall be brought low: and the crooked shall be made straight, and the rough ways plain. And all flesh shall see the salvation of God."

Meditation for the Fourth Sunday in Advent

Today in your meditation, consider the various themes drawn from the readings, and the symbolism of the fourth candle. In the readings, we again encounter the figure of John the Baptist, and his proclamation: Prepare ye the way of the Lord, make straight his paths. Saint Paul, meanwhile, reminds us that the Lord is coming, and that all judgment comes from God. What sorts of common themes can you see in these separate readings? We are not judged before the time, but Saint John the Baptist tells us that the time is at hand—and, as we have already seen, the time is *now*.

The Advent Wreath: Lighting the fourth candle

The theme of the fourth candle is Love.

Ritual for lighting the fourth candle

Step 1. Begin in your usual way, with the sign of the cross by itself or with additional prayers.
    Step 2. Read the following short verse from the Psalm 136:

> Give thanks unto the Lord; for he is good: for his mercy endureth for ever.
> Give thanks unto the God of gods: for his mercy endureth for ever.

Give thanks to the Lord of lords: for his mercy endureth for ever. Give thanks unto the God of heaven: for his mercy endureth for ever.

Step 3. Pray:

Oh God, as we light this candle, may it be for us a symbol of the Eternal Light of Thy Holy Spirit, and a sign of love for we who wander in the darkness of the lower world. *Amen.*

Light the candle.

During the meal that follows, you can encourage every member of your family to talk about love. What is the meaning of divine love? Please note: The word "mercy" in the Psalm can also be translated as love. What does it mean, then, that "his love endures forever"? You can also take love as a theme for your meditations at least some days this week.

CHAPTER TWENTY ONE

Saint Thomas's Day

December 21 is the Feast of Saint Thomas. This is another day little celebrated in America, but one with many fascinating traditional customs, worthy of a revival.

Saint Thomas himself was, as you know, one of Jesus's apostles. Like most of the Apostles, he doesn't get very many lines in the canonical Gospels. His best-known appearance comes in the Gospel of John. Jesus has risen from the dead and appeared to many, but Thomas hasn't seen him yet. He doubts the others' accounts, saying, "Unless I see in his hands the print of the nails, and place my finger in the mark of the nails, and place my hand in his side, I will not believe."

> Eight days later, his disciples were again in the house, and Thomas was with them. The doors were shut, but Jesus came and stood among them, and said, "Peace be with you."
>
> Then he said to Thomas, "Put your finger here, and see my hands; and put out your hand, and place it in my side; do not be faithless, but believing."
>
> Thomas answered him, "My Lord and my God!"
>
> Jesus said to him, "Have you believed because you have seen me? Blessed are those who have not seen and yet believe."

After the Resurrection, Thomas made his way to India, where a community of Saint Thomas Christians exists to this day. He remains the patron saint of Indian and Syrian Christians. Outside of the orthodox traditions, the Gospel of Thomas, supposedly written by him, is believed by many scholars to be the oldest of the so-called "lost Gospels." There are some who think that it, or at least parts of it, may be as old as the canonical Gospels themselves!

Saint Thomas and the Gnostic tradition

Some scholars claim to see, in the passage from John I quoted above, one side of a debate within the early Church. According to this way of looking at things, two groups within the early Church were at odds. One group followed Saint John, the other Saint Thomas, and each had its own Gospel. The Johannine group emphasized faith, while the Saint Thomas Christians emphasized the personal experience of the divine called gnosis. And so the scene in Saint John's Gospel given above is actually the Johannine Christians making fun of the Thomasites, by dismissing their ideas of personal experience. "They won't believe a word of it until they can put their hands in the Lord's wounds themselves!" We can imagine them saying this, with a loud *harrumph*.

Whether or not this is true is something I cannot say. It sounds plausible, but scholarly theories always do, until they are dismissed as outmoded nonsense by the next round of scholarly theories. It is certainly true that there were a great many Christian sects in the early days, and the very broad spectrum of groups which emphasized personal experience were called "Gnostics." They had many alternative Scriptures, including extra Gospels and other texts like the Pistis Sophia.

Gnosticism as such is outside of the scope of this book. For now, I'll only point out, in our present day as in ancient times, many people find a great deal of comfort and wisdom in the Gnostic texts. Others, myself included, find them strange and off-putting. Of all the Gnostic writings, Thomas's Gospel is the closest to the orthodox tradition, and I find many of its sayings compelling. Here is one such verse, which is especially suited to this day, as Saint Thomas Day is traditionally a day which is especially devoted to children:

> Jesus saw infants being suckled. He said to his disciples, "These infants being suckled are like those who enter the kingdom."

> They said to him, "Shall we then, as children, enter the kingdom?"
>
> Jesus said to them, "When you make the two one, and when you make the inside like the outside and the outside like the inside, and the above like the below, and when you make the male and the female one and the same, so that the male not be male nor the female female; and when you fashion eyes in the place of an eye, and a hand in place of a hand, and a foot in place of a foot, and a likeness in place of a likeness; then will you enter the kingdom."

Of course, this parallels the more familiar saying of Our Lord from the Gospel of Matthew:

> Verily I say unto you, unless ye be converted and become as little children, ye shall not enter into the Kingdom of Heaven.

Christians from the Gnostic tradition believed that their version was more complete and contained the inner, mystical side of Jesus's teachings. The orthodox disagreed, and believed the Gnostics had corrupted the original and added their own ideas to it. What do you think?

Traditional celebrations

In *Christmas in Ritual and Tradition,* Clement Miles opens the section on Saint Thomas's Day by simply saying: "Many and various are the customs and beliefs associated with the feast of Saint Thomas." In Denmark, it was the last day of school for the year; the children would bring their masters an offering of candles, and he would provide them with a feast. More interestingly, in some areas the children were made masters of their own schools for a day; testaments to their scholarship were written out, and they were given titles like "Pope" or "Emperor." In some areas, the children would lock their schoolmaster out of the building, or even tie him to his chair; he had to buy back his freedom with punch and cakes. In other regions, the schoolmaster provided his charges with hens, and let them chop their heads off.

During the age of Christendom (the "Middle Ages"), there were many such festivals, known collectively as "feasts of misrule." What they all had in common was that ordinary social customs were suspended, or upended; lords served their serfs and parents their children.

These sorts of customs are, or were, found in many parts of the world. In Rome, this is how the god Saturn was celebrated at his great feast of Saturnalia, which fell during what is now the Christmas season. These customs have a rebalancing effect on society, allowing grievances to come out and tensions to relax.

St. Thomas's Day was also a good time for magic of various kinds. In some regions, divination was practiced of the same sort as on Saint Lucy's Day, with girls performing various rituals to learn the names of their future husbands. In others, Saint Thomas himself turned up in the churchyards, riding a flaming chariot. Then all the dead men whose name had been Thomas in life rose from their graves, and accompanied the saint to the cross, which now glowed red with power. At home, the people listened for the sound of the chariot. When it was heard, they would pray to the saint for health and protection.

Saint Thomas's Day was a "smoke night" in Austria—one of the nights in which the house was blessed with incense. Elsewhere, it was also a good night to bless the animals, especially the cows. In certain parts of Germany, the cows and their barn were blessed with holy water and consecrated salt by the father of the household. Over each cow he prayed, "Saint Thomas preserve thee from all sickness." In other areas, the cows were fed with a blend of consecrated bayberries, bread, and salt, in order to avert evil and illness.

Suggestions for practice

The customs traditionally associated with this Feast Day are many and quite different from one another. Some of them are probably unavailable to us in modern America—our villages won't be crowning a boy bishop, nor will most of our children have a chance either to behead a hen or to lock out their schoolmasters. But with some creativity, we can catch the spirit of Thomas's Feast Day celebrations of old—and add some new ideas of our own.

So here are a few possibilities:

1. **The Feast of Misrule.** This requires a bit of preparation—or, at least, mental preparation. But if you have children, this might be a good day to grant them—well, if not the entire day, then a part of it in which they can run the house. (Because I'm a masochist, I just told my 10-year-old son about this, and suggested that, in the spirit of

Saint Thomas's Day, he and his baby sister could be in charge of the house tomorrow evening. My only stipulation was that he listen to me discuss the saint at dinner and share in a prayer. He was delighted by the prospect.)

2. **Divination.** Like Saint Lucy's Day, this is a good traditional day for divination practices.
3. **Meditation.** Today, consider taking some aspect from the traditions of Saint Thomas as a theme for meditation. If you are an orthodox practitioner, the appearance of Jesus to Thomas depicted in the icon at the top of this page would be appropriate. If you're interested in Gnostic ideas, consider the passage from the Gospel of Thomas I quoted above.
4. **Blessing the House and the Animals.** Most of us don't have cattle or barns, but we can still bless our homes and what animals we do have on this day. Holy water for blessing can be found at most Catholic or Orthodox churches. The stuff you find at Catholic churches these days is rather weak, as the ritual used to bless it was deliberately hobbled during the "reforms" of the last century. Weak doesn't mean useless, though; I just find its energy rather thin and pale. If you don't have it, you can take an ordinary cup of water (rainwater is best, but your tap will do), make the sign of the cross over it, and say a prayer like:

> May this water be blessed and become an agent of divine grace in the service of Thy mysteries, to drive away evil spirits and dispel sickness, so that everything in the homes and other buildings of the faithful that is sprinkled with this water may be rid of all uncleanness and freed from every harm. Through Christ Our Lord. Amen.

5. **Censing the House.** This is a good day to bless your home with incense. Suitable incenses can be found online, and you can often find incense that has already been blessed by a priest. You can also bless your own incense. You can either use the same formula that we used to bless the Advent Wreath and the Christmas tree. At the end of this section, you will also find a more advanced formula for blessing incense, which you may use at this time.

CHAPTER TWENTY TWO

The Winter of Solstice

The Winter Solstice is the longest night of the year. It marks the point in which the powers of the light have reached their nadir. And it also marks the point at which the situation reverses, and the light begins to increase. Just as it seems that darkness and cold, and winter have triumphed forever, the Sun is born again.

While many cultures throughout the world have traditionally celebrated the Winter Solstice, its observation as its own entity is fairly recent in the Christian West. Indeed, there are some who might think that the celebration of the Solstices and Equinoxes is unsuitable for Christians. Of course, they're welcome to skip this part, but I disagree. The ancient Christian teaching was that the Holy Spirit had authored two books. One was the book of Scripture, and the other was the entire world of Nature. In the cycles of the natural world, we see the working out of divine laws, and everything in Nature becomes an icon of the things in Heaven, exactly like the icons in an Orthodox Church. In the rebirth of the light in the darkest hours of winter, we see an image of the birth of Christ and of his eventual sacrifice and Resurrection.

The Sun in particular was seen as a visible image of the activity of God, as Saint Francis taught in his great prayer, the Canticle of the Sun:

> Be praised, my Lord, through all your creatures,
> especially my Lord Brother Sun,
> who brings the day; and you give light through him.
> And he is beautiful and radiant in all his splendour!
> Of you, Most High, he bears the likeness.

Before Saint Francis, Dionysius the Areopagite made the same point in his treatise *On the Divine Names*. Discussing "the Good" as one of the highest Names of God, Dionysius wrote:

> Even as our Sun, not as calculating or choosing, but by its very being, enlightens all things able to partake of its light in their own degree, so too the Good, as superior to a sun, as the archetype par excellence ... sends to all things that be, the rays of Its whole goodness, according to their capacity. By reason of these [rays] subsisted all the intelligible and intelligent essences and powers and energies.

And so I invite you to celebrate the Winter Solstice by itself, as an image in the ever-changing world of Nature of the mercy of God which abides beyond all change and time.

Please note: The exact date of the Winter Solstice varies from year to year; some years it comes as early as December 20, some years as late as December 23.

Suggestions for practice

You may already have your own methods of observing the Solstice, or else prefer to stick to those celebrations rooted in Christian tradition. I'd like to suggest three possibilities to enhance our Solstice celebrations.

1. **Tie the Solstice in with the Ember Days.** The Ember Days have just passed; and they consisted of a three-day fast. As we discussed, the Ember Days are specifically meant to attune us to the energy of the season. As the Ember Days were celebrated in a penitential manner—that is, by fasting—let the Solstice be celebrated by feasting. On this day, we can repeat the invocation of the element of Earth and of Saint

Uriel the Archangel in our meditations, focusing on gratitude for the gifts of the season. We can invite the archangel to be present with us during the day and to share in our feast.

2. **A Free Day.** While any fasting from technology should continue, let this be a day in which food-fasts are loosened; if you're abstaining from meat or drink during this season, let the fast be lifted for the day, or at least the evening. It's probably impossible to avoid work today, but make an effort to make it a "free day," in which responsibilities are loosened and conflict is avoided.

3. **The Rebirth of the Light.** The American occultist John Michael Greer has suggested a very simple Solstice celebration, and we can borrow it for our purposes. The practice consists of turning all the lights off and sitting in darkness, contemplating the season of Winter and the element of Earth. After a short while, a single candle is lit to signify the rebirth of light. We can tie this into our Esoteric Christian practice by beginning our Solstice Dinner this way. Let the family sit at the table, and let all the lights be turned off. Someone (perhaps the youngest child, if this is possible, to signify the year reborn) can then recite a suitable prayer, and the family can sit in silence for a moment. Then the candles of the Advent Wreath are lit, starting with the central white candle if there is one. Then let dinner commence.

CHAPTER TWENTY THREE

Foundations of Christian Magic: Consecrating sacramentals

One of the features of traditional Christian practice is simply the amount of *stuff* involved. Crucifixes, holy cards, statues, saints' medals, holy water, incense, consecrated oil, consecrated salt, even consecrated chalk! All of these are used in special ways in traditional Catholicism. Each is prepared in its own way and empowered with special blessings, in order to become vehicles for particular graces from God.

In traditional magic, these sorts of empowered objects are called talismans or amulets. In the Catholic tradition, they are known as *sacramentals*.

One of the great misfortunes in the modern Church has been the loss or the downplaying of the sacramentals. Often, mainstream conservative Catholics define them as simple "reminders." But a brief glance at the traditional methods for consecrating sacraments shows that they are anything but.

For example, in the *Rituale Romanum*, which contains all of the Church's traditional rituals for blessing sacramentals, there are detailed instructions for blessing the vestments, or the clothing, worn by priests, bishops, and deacons. These include prayers that every bishop, priest, or deacon clothed in these sacred vestments be strengthened and defended from all assault or temptation of wicked spirits; let them perform and celebrate your mysteries reverently and well; and let them always carry out their ministry in a devout and pleasing manner.

A simple "reminder" does not drive away evil spirits, lead men to perform the Mass with reverence; or behave in a manner pleasing to God. No: The sacramentals are objects of great spiritual power. They are material *forms* in which spiritual *force* has been invoked, in order to accomplish certain purposes which are specified in the rite of blessing.

It's worth noting that the term "sacramental" has a broader scope even than this. All of the rituals of the Church outside of the seven sacraments themselves are technically called "sacramentals." The sign of the cross is a sacramental; so is the blessing of the throat on Saint Blaise's Day; so is the making of Epiphany Water. For now, we are going to focus specifically on the art of blessing and consecrating material objects by the power of God. In the following pages, I will first present a complete ritual for consecrating incense for the purpose of blessing a house, for example, on Saint Thomas's Day. After that, we will go through the formula one step at a time and discuss how it may be applied to other sacred substances, such as oil or salt. In the Appendix, you will find a discussion of several additional sacramentals.

Please note: The ability to consecrate the sacramentals is not limited to priests, bishops or other religious. Every Christian who has been initiated by the sacrament of Baptism is linked to the current of spiritual power that has its origin in Christ. With that said, there is a difference between sacramentals and the sacraments. The sacraments do require a priest. Sacraments are said to work *ex opere operato*. This is a technical Latin term which means, basically, that as long as the priest does the ritual correctly, it will work correctly. The sacramentals are a bit different. The sacramentals work *ex opere operandis*. This is another technical term, and it means that the effect of the sacramental depends on the state of the soul of the operator. This is one of the reasons that we precede the work of consecrating a sacramental with so much preparatory work, as you will see. We want to elevate our souls, as far as possible, to the Presence of God. In the technical terms we've been using, we want to work on the Upper Astral Plane, so that we can draw power from the planes still higher.

A ritual for the censing of a house

You will want to use good-quality incense for this. Any combination of frankincense, myrrh, sandalwood, or benzoin will do nicely. Palo santo sticks are also good—you can use them by themselves, but I also like to melt a couple of grains of frankincense resin onto one. If you are using stick incense, good choices are Korean jing kwan or any of the daily incenses offered by Shoyeido.

Preparation. Set up your magical working space as usual, and put an extra bit of incense—a stick or loose resin—intended for blessing in the center of your altar or working table.

Step 1. Perform the complete opening, making sure to incorporate the Banishing Sign of the Cross.

Step 2. Optional: Depending upon the state of your own soul, you may now confess your sins in the manner described in the chapter on the Second Coming. Include the visualization if it seems appropriate; if not, you can skip it.

Step 3. Standing, with hands in the orans posture, pray the Prayer of the Holy Spirit:

> Come, Holy Spirit, fill the hearts of Thy faithful and enkindle in them the fire of Thy love.
> Send forth Thy Spirit and they shall be created, and Thou shalt renew the face of the earth.
> Let us pray.
> O God, Who didst instruct the hearts of the faithful by the light of the Holy Spirit, grant us in the same Spirit to be truly wise, and ever to rejoice in His consolation, through Christ, Our Lord. *Amen.*

Step 4. As you chant the word *Amen*, visualize a great torrent of white light pouring down from the Heavens, above you. Slowly lower your hands over the extra piece of incense, and imagine the white light of the Spirit pouring forth from your hands. Continue until the incense is filled with pure white light.

Step 5. Trace the sign of the cross over the incense, visualizing the cross in blazing white light, and say the following prayer:

> Creature of incense, I bless thee in the name of the Father, and of the Son, and of the Holy Spirit. Receive the blessing of God,

and become an agent of grace, that whatsoever is blessed by thee shall be purified of all spiritual darkness and opened to the gifts of the Holy Spirit. Through Christ Our Lord. Amen.

Step 6. Light the incense stick or place loose grains on the charcoal in your incense burner. Raise it up high and say,

> We offer thee incense, O Christ our God, for an odor of spiritual fragrance. Receive it upon your heavenly altar and send down upon us, in return, the gift of your Holy Spirit.

Step 7. Now you can use it to cleanse your home. I usually do this by drawing a small cross in the corners of every room and another very large one in the center, the last one accompanied by the words:

> Let this room be blessed in the name of the Father, and of the Son, and of the Holy Spirit, through Christ Our Lord, *Amen*.

I also draw large crosses in front of the door, with words like "

> Let this door be blessed and let all who walk through it be blessed, and let no spiritual darkness or machination of the Enemy enter into this home. Through Christ Our Lord, *Amen*.

At the end, I'll stand in a place which represents the center of the house—this is usually the kitchen—and draw another large cross, and ask for divine blessing over the whole home and all its inhabitants.

Step 8. Close in the usual way, returning to your prayer space and saying a suitable prayer, such as the Fatima Prayer or the Prayer of Saint Francis.

The formula of blessing

As a reference, here are the steps to the ritual above, which can be applied to any sacramental:

Preparation. Set up your working space. At minimum, you need a table with a crucifix and other holy objects, a vessel for holy water, and a suitable container for incense. In the center, place the object to be blessed.

Step 1. Perform the opening, with the Banishing Sign of the Cross.

Step 2. If appropriate, confess your sins.

Step 3. Use the Prayer of the Holy Spirit to call down power into the substance to be blessed through the Prayer of the Holy Spirit.

Step 4. Trace the sign of the cross over the blessed substance, visualizing it in blazing white light.

Step 5. Now, instruct the sacramental in its purpose. You can use a variation on the formula given above:

> Creature of (salt, oil, or whatever it is), I bless thee in the name of the Father, and of the Son, and of the Holy Spirit. Receive the blessing of God, and become an agent of grace, so that [here state your intention, which may be to ward off evil spirits, conduce to devotion, to bring health or good fortune.] Through Christ Our Lord, *Amen*.

Step 6. Sit in meditation for a time, visualizing the effect of your consecration, knowing that it is already accomplished, thanking God for his gifts.

Step 7. Perform the closing ritual. Close with a suitable prayer. This can be any "all-purpose" prayer; I like the Fatima Prayer and the Prayer of Saint Francis. You may wish to repeat the Our Father, pray a Psalm, or use another prayer of your choice. Always end with the sign of the cross.

You may now use the consecrated sacramental for your intended purpose.

II
CHRISTMAS

Welcome, seeker!

If you've made it this far, now is the time to celebrate. With the conclusion of Advent, our season of fasting ends, and we enter into a time of feasting.

How much feasting are we talking about? One day, after which the tree is tossed out onto the curb, and the decorations are put away! By no means. Having fasted for four weeks, we now feast for 12 straight days. Now is the time to make merry with family and friends.

In the chapters ahead, we will look at traditional customs for every day between Christmas and New Year's. You should be prepared to continue your work of prayer and meditation each of these days, and special practices are given for some. But now is the time to relax your fast, eat, drink, and be merry.

Between New Year's and Epiphany, you are largely on your own. At this point, you have all the tools you need to keep your practice going during this time. At minimum, you should read ahead through the chapters on Epiphany (January 6) and the Eve of Epiphany (January 5). These days involve a series of important practices, and you will want to be ready.

Epiphany concludes with a special ritual, an act of self-initiation into the tradition of Christian magic. It requires a few extra items, so make sure to read the section well ahead of time so that you will be prepared. You won't want to miss it.

CHAPTER TWENTY FOUR

Christmas Eve

Today is Christmas Eve! This means we've nearly made it.
 Now, unlike the Feast Days of half-forgotten saints, the celebration of Christmas Eve is one tradition that most of us do keep and keep well. For this reason, I don't think I need to spend much time telling you what it is. Instead, I'd like to discuss the traditional observance of Christmas Eve and share some thoughts on the meaning of Christmas from an esoteric perspective.

A day of fasting

Christmas Eve was traditionally a fast day. In fact, on Christmas Eve, the Advent Fast was at its most severe, beginning at sunrise and lasting through the day until the Vigil Mass. In many different countries, the fast was broken after Mass with a specific traditional meal.

 These days, especially if your children weren't raised with this idea, a severe fast on Christmas Eve is probably difficult. You can at least take steps to minimize their screen time and involve them in any housework necessary to prepare for tomorrow's holiday. Meals can be kept to a minimum until dinnertime or after evening Mass. You should certainly maintain any fasting, from technology or food, that you are doing yourself, as rigorously as possible today.

A reading from the Holy Gospel

Reading the Christmas story together as a family from Saint Luke's Gospel is a very nice way to close the day. Let's read together and talk a bit about what we're really seeing in this passage.

> And it came to pass, that in those days there went out a decree from Caesar Augustus, that the whole world should be enrolled. This enrolling was first made by Cyrinus, the governor of Syria. And all went to be enrolled, every one into his own city. And Joseph also went up from Galilee, out of the city of Nazareth into Judea, to the city of David, which is called Bethlehem: because he was of the house and family of David, To be enrolled with Mary his espoused wife, who was with child.
>
> And it came to pass, that when they were there, her days were accomplished, that she should be delivered. And she brought forth her firstborn son, and wrapped him up in swaddling clothes, and laid him in a manger; because there was no room for them in the inn. And there were in the same country shepherds watching, and keeping the night watches over their flock. And behold an angel of the Lord stood by them, and the brightness of God shone round about them; and they feared with a great fear. And the angel said to them: Fear not; for, behold, I bring you good tidings of great joy, that shall be to all the people:
>
>> For, this day, is born to you a Saviour, who is Christ the Lord, in the city of David. And this shall be a sign unto you. You shall find the infant wrapped in swaddling clothes, and laid in a manger. And suddenly there was with the angel a multitude of the heavenly army, praising God, and saying: Glory to God in the highest; and on earth peace to men of good will. And it came to pass, after the angels departed from them into heaven, the shepherds said one to another: Let us go over to Bethlehem, and let us see this word that is come to pass, which the Lord hath shewed to us.

> And they came with haste; and they found Mary and Joseph, and the infant lying in the manger. And seeing, they understood of the word that had been spoken to them concerning this child. And all that heard, wondered; and at those things that were told them by the shepherds. But Mary kept all these words, pondering them in her heart. And the shepherds returned, glorifying and praising God, for all the things they had heard and seen, as it was told unto them.

Every story in the Bible can be read on many levels, and each level itself contains many layers of meaning. Notice the opening: Caesar has ordered a census of the entire world. In ancient times, a census was no mere work of bureaucracy. Every ancient city conducted a regular census as a religious rite. In Rome, it took place every five years; in Athens, it was an annual affair. Ancient cities were not random agglomerations of people. They were religious institutions, gathered around a temple, and presided over not by men but by the city's gods. No man, then, was an island, nor could he think of himself as such. Religion pervaded the whole of life, and there was nothing like what we call the "secular sphere." The father was the head of the religion of his household, and a member of the religion of his extended family, his clan, and his tribe. If he was a citizen, he was a member of the collective body of the city. And that means that the sins of any citizen impacted every citizen. In such circumstances, it was necessary to regularly gather all the citizens together, and collectively atone for the sins of the city as a whole, reuniting the people of the city to the will of its presiding gods. This gathering was called the census; it began with the gathering of every citizen outside the city's walls and their registration with the censor. The presence of any stranger, or the absence of any citizen, would be disastrous; the censor's power was, therefore, very great at this time.

And so our Gospel begins with a census. But this isn't just any census—now the entire world is going to be enrolled. And this means that the entire world is going to make its atonement—not to the presiding gods of a house or a hearth or a clan, or even an entire city. No—for the world to make its collective atonement, it must re-unite itself to the will of the God of the entire world.

When we fast through Advent and fast severely on Christmas Eve; and when we then come together with our families, and read the story, and attend Mass if it is available to us, we re-enact this atonement in the little worlds of our own homes, communities, and churches. And if we do so, we are then blessed the next day with the birth of Christ.

CHAPTER TWENTY FIVE

Christmas Day

Gaudete, Christus est natus!

Today is Christmas Day. Today the fast ends; today our hope is fulfilled. Christ is born—born once, in Bethlehem; born again, on this day; born for all time, in our hearts. As Advent is a mirror of the entire earthly pilgrimage—a penitential sojourn through a dark land, but one lit by hope—so Christmas is an icon of heaven itself.

Today should, above all, be a day of joy. Let work be minimized. In most cases, there should be no fasting at all from meat or drink. Only in the case of addiction should fasting be rigorously followed—whether from alcohol or technology. (In my own case, it's a day to not use the internet at all, and to avoid all news and politics).

Christmas practice and meditation

Unless you come from a non-Christian culture or background, you probably have your practices covered for today. Prayer and meditation are as necessary today as any day, but I personally like to make Christmas Eve the day for my longer Christmas meditation, leaving Christmas Day for celebration.

Now is a good time to remember that Christmas is more than a single day. It's 12 days! The tree doesn't come down on the 26th, and your celebrations shouldn't end that day either.

A Christmas meditation

This may be performed either on Christmas Day or on Christmas Eve.

Preparation. In addition to the usual implements, you may want to decorate your altar with anything representing Christmas—cuttings from a Christmas tree (keep them away from open flame, or use an artificial version), a nativity scene, even Christmas ornaments or an image of Santa Claus.

Step 1. Open in the usual form, and be as deliberate as possible. Make the sign of the cross slowly and reverently, and use it to form a sphere of protection around you. You might want to use incense derived from an evergreen such as cedar or juniper, as these are at once powerful spiritual cleansers and connected with the symbolism of the season. At the opening invocation, include the words "May the Lord be with me and may the Holy Spirit guide me in my meditations on this Christmas Day."

Step 2. Enter into meditation by first relaxing your muscles and then spending a few minutes in rhythmic breathing.

Step 3. Visualize a manger filled with animals—either picture a structure of the sort one often sees in nativity scenes, but I like to picture a cave, such as one sees in older iconography. A couple is there; an older man watching over a younger woman, and the latter is about to give birth. It is, for a moment, an unpleasant scene—imagine the woman's pangs; smell the animals and their excreta; feel the irritation and rejection Joseph must have felt at being turned away from the inn. The animals bray, the woman screams; it is a scene of chaos.

And then, all is still.

The woman holds the child in her arms. From his brow, light shines forth. His foster-father—how honored is he, to be chosen as the guardian of the Word Incarnate and of the Spouse of the Holy Ghost!—falls to his knees. The animals themselves kneel. Do you know the tradition that the animals are able to speak at midnight on Christmas Day? Hear them—they know who has been born here, the Redeemer of the world; they speak, and they worship their Creator. Outside, shepherds gather, led by a host of angels. Hear their song.

Hold onto the image for as long as you like. Enter into it, feel it, let it live in your heart.

Step 4. Slowly release the image, and return to your breath for a time.

Step 5. Stand, and offer the following prayer:

> A blessed day has dawned on us, alleluia. Oh Almighty God, may the savior of the world, who came upon Earth this day, bring the Spirit of renewal to our lives and bless us during this Christmas season. *Amen.*

Step 6. Recite the words of Saint John's Gospel:

> In the beginning was the Word, and the Word was with God, and the Word was God. The same was in the beginning with God. All things were made by him; and without him was not any thing made that was made. In him was life; and the life was the light of men. And the light shineth in darkness; and the darkness comprehended it not.

Step 7. Perform the complete closing.

If you like, you can repeat this meditation throughout the Christmas season.

Merry Christmas!

The meaning of Christmas

The meaning and the purpose of the Incarnation of Christ has been a topic much debated in Christian circles over the centuries. Saint John tells us that "the Word was made flesh, and dwelt among us," but he is less clear on *why* this was so. And so the question has been debated down to the present day, with certain questions remaining open. What was the nature of the incarnate Christ? Did he have one nature, or two? Would there have been an Incarnation if there had not been a Fall? Every major branch of the faith, and every church and philosophical tradition within those branches, has its own answer to these questions.

Now, most people—and especially most Church leaders—seem to take it as a given that one of these many accounts must be the true one, and all of the others false. It is not clear that this must be so. Each Church offers its own perspective on the profound events of sacred history.

From each of these perspectives flows a set of spiritual practices and moral guidelines which shape the soul of the believer in a particular way. Calvinist Churches teach Calvinist doctrines and produce Calvinist people; Orthodox Churches teach Orthodox doctrines and produce Orthodox people. As in the old parable of the blind men and the elephant, it seems to me that each particular set of doctrines is a part of a larger truth, a truth which is ultimately unknowable. And just as athletes in different types of sport require a different set of exercises, so that the practices suitable to a marathon runner are irrelevant to a cyclist and useless to a body builder, so too different spiritual traditions require different types of practices. Catholic practices will not produce good Quakers, nor will Evangelical churches turn out Orthodox monks. From this perspective the various conflicting doctrines surrounding sacred history are there to provide a foundation for spiritual practice: nothing more, and nothing less.

What follows in this chapter is an exploration of the Incarnation from an esoteric perspective. If you are a member of one of the larger Churches, it may or may not be of interest. If, instead, you come to this work from a magical or occult background, you may find it a helpful foundation for your own spiritual practice. As always, it is put forward here as a model for consideration, not doctrine demanding belief.

That said, let us start where we must start. In the Beginning ...

The creation

> In the beginning, God created the Heavens and the Earth.
> On the Fifth Day, he created Man. Male and female created He them, in His Own Image created He them.

Or, another way:

> The Lord God formed man of dust from the ground, and breathed into his nostrils the breath of life; and man became a living being. And later, the Lord God caused a deep sleep to fall upon the man, and while he slept took one of his ribs and closed up its place with flesh; and the rib which the Lord God had taken from the man he made into a woman and brought her to the man.

* * *

And so we have two different accounts of the creation of Mankind. These two do not contradict one another. We are to understand that, in one sense, the material form of Man comes late in the sequence of Creation. God first brings forth land, which is the mineral creation; and then plants and trees, the vegetable creation; and then the animal creation. Only after these things are accomplished can the form of Man come into being.

This is, according to our science, a fairly accurate summary of how the events actually unfolded. It is also a model of the Journey of Return, by which every soul. According to teachings found in esoteric schools such as the Rosicrucian tradition and the Druid Revival, every soul has its origin in God. It then sinks into matter, as far as the mineral creation, the lowest possible created thing. From there it begins the Journey of Return, making its way step by step through the plant and animal orders, until it finally incarnates in human form.

There is a reason that it must be so. The Eternal Man is nothing other than Christ Himself, True Man and True God. And Christ is the Divine Mind. To be truly the Divine Mind, Christ must know all things. And to truly know is to know by experience. Christ is thus present to all things, knowing all things, experiencing all things, suffering all things. This is how we may know that the Journey of Return is always present to all beings, no matter how low they have sunk: Because Christ is always present to them, urging them upward.

Now, even as Man comes last in the order of creation, he also comes first. The ancients taught that all of the visible and sensible things that we perceive are shaped and governed by the invisible and intelligible Ideas. Those Ideas are thoughts in the Mind of God, ever shaping our visible reality. This is what is meant by "The Lord created the Heavens and the Earth." The Earth refers, here, to sensible things, and the Heavens to intelligible things.

In the second account in Genesis, we learn of the Idea of Man, and of his structure. "Male and female created He them, in his own image created He them." By the male is signified the *Nous* or Intellect, and by the Female, the Psyche or Soul. By the image of God, the presence within Man of the Divine Spark: the inner being in all of us that derives from the very being of God.

The Man and the Woman are not two individuals, but one, the archetypal Human Being. Each person has within him Adam, and Eve, and the Image of God.

The Fall

> Now the serpent was more subtle than any other wild creature that the Lord God had made. He said to the woman, "Did God say, 'You shall not eat of any tree of the garden'?" And the woman said to the serpent, "We may eat of the fruit of the trees of the garden; but God said, 'You shall not eat of the fruit of the tree which is in the midst of the garden, neither shall you touch it, lest you die.'" But the serpent said to the woman, "You will not die. For God knows that when you eat of it your eyes will be opened, and you will be like God, knowing good and evil." So when the woman saw that the tree was good for food, and that it was a delight to the eyes, and that the tree was to be desired to make one wise, she took of its fruit and ate; and she also gave some to her husband, and he ate. Then the eyes of both were opened, and they knew that they were naked; and they sewed fig leaves together and made themselves aprons.

The serpent is the desiring part of the soul, the appetite or *epithymia*. It now turns its gaze toward the material creation. This is why it is said that the tree is "good for food" and a "delight to the eyes." And the serpent which sheds its skin and crawls on its belly is the image of the life lived in the material world of life and death, generation and corruption. The serpent also represents that which is outside of the soul and toward which the soul looks: In this case, rather than keeping its eye fixed on the Heavenly World of God and the Angels, it finds itself tempted by the things of the material world. Thus the soul turns toward its lower parts, the appetites, which are bound up with the body and material things. It then draws after it the *Nous*. Every part is now drawn into material creation. The Human Being, formerly altogether spiritual, now "makes itself an apron," which is to say, it clothes itself in a material body. Soon, God himself will create for them garments of skin. This completes the process of the descent into Matter.

And the fruit of the Tree will indeed make one wise. But that comes later.

> Then the Lord God said, "Behold, the man has become like one of us, knowing good and evil; and now, lest he put forth his hand and take also of the tree of life, and eat, and live for ever"—therefore the Lord God sent him forth from the garden of Eden, to till the ground

from which he was taken. He drove out the man; and at the east of the garden of Eden he placed the cherubim, and a flaming sword which turned every way, to guard the way to the tree of life.

It is said that, at this time, Sin and Death entered the world. In ancient writing and iconography these are proper nouns, names. It could as well be said that the Human Being, Adam-Eve, enters the World of Sin and Death. By "sin" is signified karma, actions which bind us to matter. "Sin" is also a proper name: The name of Satan or Lucifer, the power of this world which seeks to keep us enthralled in matter, sin, and suffering. By "death" is signified death as we commonly understand it, but two other things. The first is Death Himself, or Hades. The second is the Underworld over which Hades presides, which is also called Hades. In early Christian writings and to this day in the Eastern Church, "Hell" and "Hades" are distinct, and so are Death and Lucifer. Entering into the world of Sin, mankind is subject unto Hades, the ruler of the world of the Dead.

Here is the secret teaching, which was at the heart of the ancient Mysteries:

We are all, already, in the world of the Dead.

The descent into Hades is also the descent into the material body. The soil wherein the dead are buried is the Mineral Kingdom, the kingdom of raw matter, whose ruler is Death. When we depart our bodies at Death our spirits abide for a time as ghosts in the Underworld, and then return to material bodies, again and again and again. Soma is sema: The body itself is the tomb. This will go on until we can become free. But how? Let us return to our story.

The genealogy

On Earth, ages pass, and many generations are begotten.

> Abraham was the father of Isaac, and Isaac the father of Jacob, and Jacob the father of Judah and his brothers, and Judah the father of Perez and Zerah by Tamar, and Perez the father of Hezron, and Hezron the father of Ram, and Ram the father of Ammin'adab, and Ammin'adab the father of Nahshon, and Nahshon the father of Salmon, and Salmon the father of Bo'az by Rahab, and Bo'az the father of Obed by Ruth, and Obed the father of Jesse, and Jesse the father of David the king.

And David was the father of Solomon by the wife of Uri'ah and Solomon the father of Rehobo'am, and Rehobo'am the father of Abi'jah, and Abi'jah the father of Asa, and Asa the father of Jehosh'aphat, and Jehosh'aphat the father of Joram, and Joram the father of Uzzi'ah, 9 and Uzzi'ah the father of Jotham, and Jotham the father of Ahaz, and Ahaz the father of Hezeki'ah, and Hezeki'ah the father of Manas'seh, and Manas'seh the father of Amos, and Amos the father of Josi'ah, and Josi'ah the father of Jechoni'ah and his brothers, at the time of the deportation to Babylon.

And after the deportation to Babylon: Jechoni'ah was the father of She-al'ti-el, and She-al'ti-el the father of Zerub'babel, and Zerub'babel the father of Abi'ud, and Abi'ud the father of Eli'akim, and Eli'akim the father of Azor, and Azor the father of Zadok, and Zadok the father of Achim, and Achim the father of Eli'ud, and Eli'ud the father of Elea'zar, and Elea'zar the father of Matthan, and Matthan the father of Jacob, and Jacob the father of Joseph the husband of Mary, of whom Jesus was born, who is called Christ.

In the genealogy is, perhaps, signified a literal genealogy, or perhaps not. Its inner meaning is the cycle of reincarnation. Abraham begins the process, by his willing assent to Divine Commandment. In his willingness to give Isaac to God is signified the turning of the soul toward spiritual things; in God's freeing of Isaac, the beginning of the end of subjection to the rule of Death. In the genealogy that follows we see the long cycle of reincarnation that continues from the beginning of a spiritual journey to its culmination. Abraham is Adam, or a participant in the Human Idea which is called Adam–Eve and sometimes, in Kabbalistic writings, Adam Cadmon.

The Annunciation

And in the sixth month, the angel Gabriel was sent from God into a city of Galilee, called Nazareth,

To a virgin espoused to a man whose name was Joseph, of the house of David; and the virgin's name was Mary.

And the angel being come in, said unto her: Hail, full of grace, the Lord is with thee: blessed art thou among women.

Who having heard, was troubled at his saying, and thought with herself what manner of salutation this should be.

> And the angel said to her: Fear not, Mary, for thou hast found grace with God.
> Behold thou shalt conceive in thy womb, and shalt bring forth a son; and thou shalt call his name Jesus.
>
> He shall be great, and shall be called the Son of the most High; and the Lord God shall give unto him the throne of David his father; and he shall reign in the house of Jacob for ever.
> And of his kingdom there shall be no end.
> And Mary said to the angel: How shall this be done, because I know not man?
> And the angel answering, said to her: The Holy Ghost shall come upon thee, and the power of the most High shall overshadow thee. And therefore also the Holy which shall be born of thee shall be called the Son of God.

Before we get to Jesus, we have to start with Mary. In Catholic tradition Mary is given many titles. Among these are: Immaculate Conception, Model for Christians, Virgin Pure, Mother of God, the New Eve.

All of these titles have a special spiritual significance. By "the New Eve" we understand that Mary *is* Eve. The complete Human Being is called Adam–Eve, and is also called Mary–Jesus. The journey from Adam–Eve to Mary-Jesus through the stories of kingship, exile, conquest and redemption found in the Old Testament is the archetype of the journey of the human soul. This is why she is called "Model for Christians." Turning toward matter, the soul descends into matter. Assenting to Divine Command, it begins its conquest of matter. Purified and divinized, it is born free of karma: this is the "Immaculate Conception." The soul may now "give birth" to the Christ, which is to the *Nous*, the higher part of the spirit which is above Soul. This is why she is called "Virgin," because she signifies the soul which has turned its gaze away from the things of generation in the material creation and toward the eternal things of the noetic and divine realms.

As Mary is the New Eve, Jesus is the New Adam. As Eve is born of Adam's rib, Jesus is born of Mary's womb. Neither has a second parent. Eve is called "Wife of Adam" to signify that Adam–Eve represents the soul in its downward journey into materiality. But Jesus is called "Son of Mary" to signify that here the soul is on its upward journey, away from generation.

The serpent, meanwhile, who tempted our first parents, is now replaced by Saint Joseph, the guardian of the Holy Family. Saint Joseph represents the strength of the soul, the part called the *thymos*, which is now put into the service of the *Nous*, rather than acting as a willing conspirator with the appetites. In addition to being guardian of the Holy Family, Saint Joseph is also the patron of the Universal Church. Now, the Universal Church is more than a particular human institution. The Church as a whole includes all of the true particular churches, and from our perspective that very much includes the esoteric, the magical and Gnostic traditions. Remember that the Church is also called "the body of Christ." Real bodies have many parts, and truly resemble forests more than statues. As such, the Universal Church represents the redemption of the body and of matter as a whole. This is the ultimate purpose both of Adam-Eve's descent into matter and the incarnation of Christ through the Holy Spirit and the Virgin Mary.

The Incarnation

> In those days a decree went out from Caesar Augustus that all the world should be enrolled. This was the first enrollment, when Quirin'i-us was governor of Syria. And all went to be enrolled, each to his own city. And Joseph also went up from Galilee, from the city of Nazareth, to Judea, to the city of David, which is called Bethlehem, because he was of the house and lineage of David, to be enrolled with Mary, his betrothed, who was with child. And while they were there, the time came for her to be delivered. And she gave birth to her first-born son and wrapped him in swaddling cloths, and laid him in a manger, because there was no place for them in the inn.

We come now to the birth of Christ. The author, Luke, begins with a census. As we wrote in the last chapter, in ancient times the census was not a mere bureaucratic venture, but a religious rite. During the census, every citizen would return to the city of their birth and offer repentance for their sins to the God of that city. An Athenian returned to Athens, and repents of his sins to Athena and Hephaestus; a Spartan returned to Sparta, and repented to Zeus; and so on. Every city has its particular God.

But now the census is to survey "the entire world." What this means is that "the particular God" in question is not the local God of this city or that city, but the God of Gods, the God of the whole world. From the Beginning He has been hidden. Now, in a lonely corner of the Roman Empire, He reveals Himself.

He is born in a manger, with animals; and this is also called a cave. The cave is an ancient image of the material order, and His birth there signifies the beginning of the return journey from the material creation to the spiritual order. By the animals it is signified that the soul which descends into matter descends at least as far as the level of the beasts, though some say lower, to the level of vegetables; and others say lower still, all the way to the mineral creation. Perhaps it depends on the soul.

In ancient times, it was said that animals could speak at midnight on Christmas. This reminds us that the noetic power is present in the animal creation as well, and the animals are also on the Journey of Return.

Later, Jesus, which is to say, the awakened *Nous* in the Human Being, will return to the Garden, which is now called Gethsemane. And he will ascend the Tree of Life, which is the Cross. Descending, he will break open the doors of Hades, which is to say, he will model and become the Journey of Return, so that all who follow after Him may no longer die. But that is a story for another night.

CHAPTER TWENTY SIX

Saint Stephen's Day

December 26, the day after Christmas, is Saint Stephen's Day. Back at the beginning of Advent, I wrote that it's even harder to imagine Americans partying for 12 days straight than it is to imagine them fasting for four weeks. Saint Stephen's Day, the first day after Christmas itself, is not much kept in this country—indeed, some treat it as the day to take down the Christmas decorations and throw out the tree!

Well, it's high time that changed. Let's talk about Saint Stephen, his traditional observances, and how we might celebrate his Feast.

Stephen, Protomartyr

Saint Stephen was the first Christian martyr. His story is related thusly in the Acts of the Apostles:

> And Stephen, full of grace and power, did great wonders and signs among the people. Then some of those who belonged to the synagogue of the Freedmen (as it was called), and of the Cyre'nians, and of the Alexandrians, and of those from Cili'cia and Asia, arose and disputed with Stephen. But they could not withstand the wisdom and the Spirit with which he spoke. Then they secretly

instigated men, who said, "We have heard him speak blasphemous words against Moses and God." And they stirred up the people and the elders and the scribes, and they came upon him and seized him and brought him before the council, and set up false witnesses who said, "This man never ceases to speak words against this holy place and the law; for we have heard him say that this Jesus of Nazareth will destroy this place, and will change the customs which Moses delivered to us." And gazing at him, all who sat in the council saw that his face was like the face of an angel.

Stephen speaks at length and attempts to persuade the council to accept Jesus. But they refuse:

> Now when they heard these things they were enraged, and they ground their teeth against him. But he, full of the Holy Spirit, gazed into heaven and saw the glory of God, and Jesus standing at the right hand of God; and he said, "Behold, I see the Heavens opened, and the Son of man standing at the right hand of God." But they cried out with a loud voice and stopped their ears and rushed together upon him. Then they cast him out of the city and stoned him; and the witnesses laid down their garments at the feet of a young man named Saul. And as they were stoning Stephen, he prayed, "Lord Jesus, receive my spirit." And he knelt down and cried with a loud voice, "Lord, do not hold this sin against them." And when he had said this, he fell asleep.

It is likely that Stephen's veneration goes back to the 1st century, and that this is why the story of his martyrdom was detailed at such length in the book of Acts.

Traditional practices

The traditional practices surrounding Saint Stephen's Day are many and interesting. Returning to *Christmas in Ritual and Tradition*, we learn:

> In Tyrol, this is traditionally a time for the blessing of water and salt. The water is sprinkled in the fields to avert the influences of witches and evil spirits, and bread dipped in it is given to cattle. Horses are given consecrated salt and grains. Horses were also bled

on this day in many regions, back when bleeding was still good for health. In still other regions, horses decked with ribbons were raced about the town, or through the Church, and blessed and exorcised by priests. In Sweden, it was the custom at one time to take horses to water at exactly 1:00 in the morning on Saint Stephen's Day, with a reward for whoever arrived first.

It was also a common practice on this day for young men to go from town to town, before dawn, singing raucously. For whatever reason, they were given beer or liquor for their trouble, which is a common theme in traditions of this sort.

Of course, it is just this sort of tradition that is preserved in America in the trick-or-treating that we do on Halloween. In earlier times, trick-or-treating was apparently seen as a fine way to celebrate more or less any holiday, and it was an all-ages affair. God send the day may come again!

In the British Isles, there was an odd variation on this theme which persisted into the modern era and has survived in certain parts of the United States. This is the "wren day" custom, in which men dressed in mummer's garb would kill a wren and go door to door demanding money for the poor bird's funeral. The money was then used to throw a party for the entire town.

Suggestions for practice

With few exceptions, most of us won't have a chance to race our horses about the village at 1 am in the morning, or to dress up as mummers and bury a wren. That said, we can still incorporate some of the traditional methods of celebrating Saint Stephen's Day.

First, if you have horses, and I know some of you do, this would be a good traditional day to bless them. Give them consecrated bread, salt, and holy water—and you can consecrate these yourself, if you like.

Of course, most of us don't have horses. But most of us have family or friends. So do what they did in the old days—have a party! Invite your friends and extended family, and continue the Christmas celebration by exchanging gifts outside of the immediate family.

Saint Stephen's Day meditation

We should also take the time to honor Saint Stephen by reflecting on his story and his martyrdom.

Today in meditation, read the discussion of Saint Stephen from the Acts of the Apostles, Chapters 6 and 7. Enter into meditation in the usual way, and explore these ideas in your mind. This can take any form you like—you can visualize the martyrdom as an event taking place before your eyes. You can contemplate the meaning of his martyrdom, or of any particular element of the story—what does it mean that his face showed like an angel? What is the meaning of the long discussion of Jewish history which precedes his martyrdom in Acts 7? You can use either of these methods or something else entirely. Follow the thought for as long as possible, and then release it with a prayer to God, and perhaps a resolution to face the challenges of life as Stephen faced his accusers. Close the meditation in the usual way.

CHAPTER TWENTY SEVEN

Saint John's Day

December 27 is the Feast of Saint John the Evangelist. This is another feast not often enough acknowledged in the contemporary American Church, but it's quite an interesting one. Falling just after the Nativity of Our Lord, it is necessarily linked to the Winter Solstice. On the other side of the year, June 24 is the Feast of Saint John the Baptist. The name John, *Yohannon*, means "Graced by God," or, rather, by *Yahweh*. As "Grace" is a way of saying "Divine Power," and the name "Yahweh" specifically refers to God's nature as the source of life and existence, we can see that both saints called John are earthly embodiments of the highest Divine Power. From the shared name of the two saints, John and the dates of their feasts, we see that these two are connected, and that they bear a connection to the Sun and the cycle of the year. Notice, too, that the Feast of John the Baptist is at the Summer Solstice, when the light, which is at its maximum, begins to decrease, while John the Evangelist is born at the Winter Solstice, when the dim light is yet growing again. There is much here that could be unpacked in meditation. Indeed, there is an entire tradition of Johannine Christianity, of which the largest contemporary example is a Gnostic organization called the Apostolic Johannite Church.

Of course, Saint John is one of the four evangelists, the author of the Gospel of John, the Apocalypse of John, and several New Testament epistles. It's very hard to overstate the importance of Saint John. He is referred to as "the Beloved Disciple," and it is to his care that the Blessed Virgin Mary is entrusted by Our Lord Himself from the cross. He is also invoked as the patron of love, friendship, and authors. In iconography, he is connected with an eagle, as Saint Mark is connected with a lion, Luke with a bull, and Matthew with a man. These symbols suggest the four faces of the Cherubim, but they also symbolize the four cardinal signs of the Zodiac. Mark, the lion, is connected with the sign of Leo; Matthew, the Man, with Aquarius; Luke, the bull, with Taurus. Saint John's Eagle, meanwhile, symbolizes Scorpio. Unlike the other signs, Scorpio has three images, not just one. It can manifest as a scorpion lying under a rock in the realm of Matter and stinging all those who try to expose it to the Sun; as a poisonous snake, slithering through the waters of the Astral realm; or an eagle soaring above those waters in the sunlight of the spirit.

Saint John and the wine cup

Saint John is often depicted with a wine cup, out of which a small snake or dragon emerges. This comes from an incident in the later life of the saint. It seems that, while at Ephesus, Saint John was offered a cup of poisoned wine. But the saint blessed the cup, and the poison crawled right out of it in the form of a snake.

For this reason, Saint John's Day has been the traditional day to bless wine, or sometimes cider. This consecrated wine can then be used year-round for any purpose you can imagine—to promote health, prevent attacks of witches and evil spirits, and so on. A few drops can be added to ordinary table wine in order to turn it into a magical beverage.

A ritual for the blessing of wine

Preparation. In the Feast of Saint Thomas, we learned the formula for blessing. We can use the same ritual to perform the blessing of wine on Saint John's Day. The difference is that you should have a cup, bottle, or other vessel of wine on your altar or prayer table. An icon of Saint John would not be out of place, either.

Perform the blessing according to the template given in Foundations of Christian Magic 5: Blessings and Consecrations.

At Step 4, you may use the following formula: Trace the Sign of the Cross over the wine, and instruct it as follows:

> Creature of wine, I bless thee in the name of the Father, and of the Son, and of the Holy Spirit. Receive the blessing of God, and become an agent of divine grace, that whoever shall drink of thee will receive healing and purification. Through Christ Our Lord, *Amen.*

If you prefer, you can also substitute a longer, traditional blessing, at this point. Every time you see a +, make the Sign of the Cross, visualizing it in blazing white fire descending into the wine.

> If it please you, Lord God, bless + and consecrate + this vessel of wine (or any other beverage) by the power of your right hand; and grant that, through the merits of Saint John, apostle and evangelist, all your faithful who drink of it may find it a help and a protection. As the blessed John drank the poisoned potion without any ill effects, so may all who today drink the blessed wine in his honor be delivered from poisoning and similar harmful things. And as they offer themselves body and soul to you, may they obtain pardon of all their sins; through Christ Our Lord. *Amen.*
>
> Lord, bless + this creature of wine, so that it may be a health-giving medicine to all who use it; and grant by your grace that all who taste of it may enjoy bodily and spiritual health in calling on your holy name; through Christ Our Lord. *Amen.*
>
> May the blessing of Almighty God, Father, Son, + and Holy Spirit, come on this wine (or any other beverage) and remain always. *Amen.*

Sprinkle the wine three times with holy water; if using an open container, you can add three drops of holy water directly to the wine itself.

Continue with the usual closing.

Meditation for Saint John's Day

For Saint John's Day, an appropriate meditation should be drawn from the works attributed to him. The traditional reading in both the Catholic and Anglican churches is John 21:19–24. This is an option, and in both of these churches the Collect is either the following or something like it:

> O Lord, let the Church be enlightened by the teachings of Your blessed apostle and evangelist John, so that she may enjoy Your everlasting gifts.

The Collect could be offered as a prayer after the reading. There are also a number of Gnostic and other mystical texts attributed to Saint John. I don't personally make much use of these, as they tend to come from the tradition of Sethian Gnosticism, which has never much interested me. But if they appeal to you, today would be a good day for them!

CHAPTER TWENTY EIGHT

The Feast of the Holy Innocents

December 28 is the Feast of the Holy Innocents. It is also known as Childermas.

The "Holy Innocents" are the children who were killed by King Herod after the Christ Child escaped with his family to Egypt. As we learn from Saint Matthew's Gospel, the three magi came from the east to worship the child, but they were warned in a dream not to return to King Herod.

> Then Herod, when he saw that he had been tricked by the wise men, was in a furious rage, and he sent and killed all the male children in Bethlehem and in all that region who were two years old or under, according to the time which he had ascertained from the wise men. 17 Then was fulfilled what was spoken by the prophet Jeremiah:
>
> > A voice was heard in Ramah,
> > wailing and loud lamentation,
> > Rachel weeping for her children;
> > she refused to be consoled,
> > because they were no more.

Childermas in tradition

In Spain and other Spanish-speaking countries, Childermas is celebrated in much the same way as April Fool's Day in America. It's a day of pranks and general mischief-making.

Another custom, found elsewhere in the world, allows the youngest child in the house to be the king or queen for the day. The youngest gets to decide the day's activities, including food, drink, activities, and entertainment.

We've encountered these ideas before. These sorts of celebrations are called "feasts of misrule," and they take various forms throughout the world, as we've seen. These sorts of customs temporarily invert the normal social order. They serve to both let everybody "blow off steam," and to affirm the natural order—once it has been re-established!

Finally, it's worth mentioning that according to old English tradition, whatever day of the week Childermas falls on becomes unlucky for the rest of the year to follow. No new projects should be started on Childermas itself, and you might want to take extra precautions during that day for the year that follows. This is true even if you don't "believe in" bad luck—it's a common experience that when we tap into an old tradition like this one, we end up with the bad as well as the good!

Suggestions for practice

1. If you're up for it, you might consider letting your children know that today is like April Fool's Day, and allow them to get away with whatever little pranks they like. (If you don't have children, this is one time to count your blessings.) If you've had enough of misrule for one season, of course, you may simply decide that this one doesn't apply to you.
2. Again, if you have children, allow your youngest to be king or queen for the day. If you keep it within reason, they will have fun with it.
3. If you don't have children, this might be a good day to donate or volunteer at a children's charity, or to spend time with nieces, nephews, or children of your friends. Treat it as an offering or act of almsgiving (see Foundations of Christian Magic 3: Almsgiving and Offerings, under the Second Week of Advent), and give your parents, friends, or siblings a little break.

Prayer and meditation for Childermas

Here is a traditional prayer for the Holy Innocents:

> Ye Holy Innocents, blest Babes, earliest martyrs of Jesus Christ, the King of martyrs, how bright a life was won by that sharp death! Beautiful little martyrs of the holy Child, your eyes soon closed upon the dull mists of earth, to open upon untold glories. Bitter and short the passage, but oh, how passing sweet the end! How sweet to have died for Him Who came to give His life for you! Pray for me, ye stainless ones, before the Throne, that I too, unworthy and wayward as I am, may come to be with those who follow the Lamb whithersoever He goeth. Most Holy Child Jesus, save Thy children.

In meditation, you may bring to mind the verses cited above from the Gospel of Matthew and explore their meaning. No, it isn't an easy thing to contemplate, but children do die before their time in this sorrowful world. Why does this happen? What does it mean for the innocent ones, as described in the prayer above, to stand before the throne of God and intercede on our behalf?

It is a difficult truth for us to bear, but an untimely death is not the worst thing that can befall us on this Earth. The sorrow that follows is not the sorrow of the innocent ones whose souls are now in Heaven. The sorrow is entirely ours, who are left here without them.

CHAPTER TWENTY NINE

Saint Thomas Becket

December 29 is the Feast of Saint Thomas Becket, or Thomas à Becket as he is often known.

Thomas Becket was a medieval English priest who eventually rose to become the Archbishop of Canterbury. In the 1160s, he came into conflict with the king of England, Henry II. In those days, the churches were like a separate society, with their own lands, their own laws, even their own peasants and their own armies. As king of England, Henry wanted more control over the churches in his land, and Thomas, the most powerful priest in England, opposed him. The conflict came to a head when a group of bishops crowned Henry's son heir to the throne, which violated Thomas's privileges as Archbishop of Canterbury. Thomas excommunicated the renegade bishops. Hearing about the excommunication, Henry uttered the (quite literally) fatal words: "Will no one rid me of this meddlesome priest?"

Well, "plausible deniability" is a term that modern governments use when they want to do something sneaky but don't want to be able to be held responsible. Apparently, it was a thing in the Middle Ages as well. Henry didn't officially order Thomas's execution, but his knights got the idea. One evening, four of them came to Thomas in Canterbury and demanded that he submit to the authority of the king. Thomas refused, and the knights came again, this time with swords drawn, demanding that Thomas submit. Again, Thomas refused, saying, "For the name of Jesus and the protection of the church, I am ready to embrace death."

The knights fell upon Thomas and killed him. Accounts from the time tell us that his head was broken open, and his brains scattered by the knights' fifth companion, a traitor priest.

We may suppose that the knights believed that their work had been accomplished. But it is the way of things divine that what seems like the triumph of darkness is in fact the beginning of its defeat. As a martyr to the faith, Thomas was quickly recognized as a saint, being canonized Saint Thomas by the Pope in 1173. A year later, Henry himself was forced to finally submit to Thomas in humble penance before the archbishop's tomb. The knights who assassinated Thomas were eventually excommunicated, only being restored to the Church after serving as holy warriors in the Holy Land for 14 years.

And that was only the beginning. Miracles very quickly began to gather around him, and his tomb became a place of pilgrimage. At one point, it was even common for pilgrims to take "Saint Thomas's Water," which was a healing potion made from water mixed with the remains of Saint Thomas's blood!

Saint Thomas Becket—Breaking Open the Head

"Breaking Open the Head" comes from a 2002 book on shamanism by Daniel Pinchbeck. The term comes from the Bwiti people of Western Africa, who use a psychedelic drink called iboga to open the doors of perception, allowing them to contact spirits and work in the Otherworld.

In the Western tradition, we forgo the use of psychotropics and instead work to "break open the head" through the patient's development of the spiritual faculties. And yet, the concept of "breaking open the head" is not foreign to us. We have seen that the head, in traditional psychic anatomy, is the seat of the Intellect or *Nous*, the "eye of the soul," which is able to perceive spiritual realities directly. This is related to the idea of the "third eye" from Eastern traditions. While no reference to the third eye has survived in his writings, we know from other sources (Origen) that the philosopher Plato was aware of the third eye as well.

Saint Thomas's story is historical. It really happened, and at the level of the mundane concerns of the world it was a political assassination. At the same time, if we're going to be honest historians, we know that, after his death, miracles began to happen. People visited his tomb and were cured of many illnesses.

At another level, the level of magical philosophy, Saint Thomas's story is myth, and the myth is precisely that of breaking open the head reported in Pinchbeck's book. In the shamanic traditions from around the world, a new shaman frequently encounters spirits who dismember the new shaman, tearing him apart in some way. In some cultures, both good shamans and evil witches retain the ability to send forth their heads at night.

And notice that the death of Becket came on orders—or, at least, *suggestions*—from the king himself. It's hard for Americans to understand kings. On the one hand, many of us retain a fascination with the British crown; at the same time, our national myth is built around the rebellion against a king. On some level, we all regard kings as tyrannical by nature.

The traditional understanding of kings and kingship is very different. I'm not asking you to become a monarchist, by the way; I'm an American, too, after all, and my faith is in the republic. But we need to understand that, the world over, the king is not merely a government official or even an administrator. The king symbolizes the whole people, and, in a way, the whole world. He invariably has magic power. In many ancient societies, the king was also the chief priest.

And so, on one level, we can see King Henry the Second as a political tyrant ordering the assassination of his rival. At another level, he is a magical initiator who sends forth the knights, his servant spirits, to guide Thomas Becket in his initiation. The knights order Becket to submit to the king. This is an invitation. He is given a chance to turn back, return to the temporal world, and abandon the sunlit heights of the spirit. Steadfast, he refused, and the knights, spirits, set to the true work of initiation. Becket's head is broken open. And now the man, Thomas Becket, dies to this world, and a new spiritual power, Saint Thomas Becket, is born.

Suggestions for practice

I don't have a great deal to offer in the way of traditions and customs for Saint Thomas Becket Day. Perhaps the English have some. In the meantime, this might be a great opportunity to create some new traditions of your own. At minimum, you can discuss the story of the saint's life and death with your family and what it means. If you're feeling morbid, you might make some variation on "Saint Thomas Water," hopefully using a red juice like pomegranate juice in place of actual blood. Add ice cubes, lime juice and vodka to make a sacramental fit for the adults in the house. Have fun and see what you come up with!

Meditation for the Feast of Saint Thomas Becket

As you enter into meditation, imagine the scene at the cathedral in Canterbury, nearly 900 years ago. See the monk kneeling in prayer; see the knights enter. They are four, representing the four elements of the material world, and they are accompanied by a priest, representing the fifth element of Spirit. They issue the king's orders. Becket refuses. They set upon him, and break open his skull.

See Becket's spirit, freed of the body. See the visitors who begin to approach his shrine, one or two becoming a trickle, the trickle becoming a flood. See them healed of all that ails them. As you meditate, I invite you to consider both the historical events and the mythical interpretation I have offered of them. You may offer the following prayer.

> Saint Thomas Becket, aid us in opening the eye of our souls, that we may begin to perceive the spiritual world directly, as you do, through Jesus Christ Our Lord. Saint Thomas Becket, pray for us. *Amen.*

CHAPTER THIRTY

The Holy Family

December 30 is dedicated to the Holy Family of Jesus, Mary, and Joseph.

This is a fairly recent feast. Some sources claim that it has been celebrated in certain regions for several hundred years; others, that it only began in the 19th century, in Canada. In either case, it was only added to the general calendar in 1921. Even then, it was celebrated after Epiphany for nearly 50 years. Its current date was only established in 1969!

This presents us with a great opportunity. Throughout this book, we've emphasized the importance of history and tradition. But real history is a continuing process, and real tradition unites past, present and future. Since the Feast of the Holy Family is so recent, not very many traditions have gathered around it. That means that, here, we have a chance to create our own customs and make our own contribution to the great tradition.

The Holy Family as the ideal of the family

Above all, the Holy Family is the ideal of the family itself, the model of what every family should be. Within the Holy Family, each member selflessly fulfills their duty to the other two, to the family as a whole, and to God. This is more than a set of prescriptions. This is Justice. In contemporary thinking, the word "justice" often refers to punishment by the government, and sometimes to the idea that the government ought to punish one part of its citizens on behalf of another part. The ancient understanding of Justice is very different. For Plato and Aristotle, and for the Church which learned from them, Justice means *properly ordered relationships*. A family in which each member serves the others and the family as a whole is a family in which the principle of Justice is established.

Notice how the Holy Family both confirms and inverts our usual understanding of proper order within the family. Saint Joseph is the guardian of the Holy Family and its head on Earth, but in Heaven, his wife, Mary, is ultimately set over him. Jesus is their child, and we learn from the Gospel that "he submitted to them in all things." But as he is the Word of God Himself, he is ultimately set over his earthly parents, as he is set over all things.

It's worth noting in passing that many Christians these days are fixated on the idea of women, all women, submitting entirely to their husbands. Discussions of this have become more common in recent years, probably in reaction to the excesses of feminism in the previous decade. Such is the way of things on Earth; all things give way to their opposites. It is true that Saint Paul wrote that a wife ought to be subject to her husband, but it is also true that he commands each to obey the other. Saint John Chrysostom expanded on this, pointing out that both the body and the property of each spouse belongs, ultimately, to the other.

I'm not a big fan of people who try to organize other people's personal lives for them, and nothing is more personal than marriage. And so I have no intention of telling you what your marriage should look like. What I want to point to instead is the principle at work here. As we have seen, that is the principle of Justice. Justice means everything is rightly ordered, and every part does its duty to the whole and to God. What that means in your life and that of your family is for you and your spouse to determine.

But what of those without children, or without spouses, or whose birth families are dead or estranged? Is this feast simply not meant for them?

By no means. Of course, both as the individual powers of Saint Joseph, Saint Mary, and Our Lord Himself, each is available to all. But as the family of two parents and one child is the simplest of human social groups, the Holy Family becomes the model and ideal type of all human organizations, from a Church or a charity to an amateur sports league or a group of friends gathered at a pub.

Beyond this, the Holy Family can be seen as an ideal of the soul itself. We have already seen that the soul consists of three parts: the *Nous* or Intellect, the *Thymos* or Heart, and the *Epithymia* or desire. Each member of the Holy Family can be seen to represent a part of the soul, perfected in itself and working together in perfect harmony with the other parts. In her total obedience to the Will of God, Mary represents the perfection of the *Epithymia* or desire, whose proper desire is for God only. As the guardian of the Holy Family, Saint Joseph represents the perfection of the *Thymos*, which is directed not toward conflict with others or worldly honors, but to safeguarding that which is good and holy. Christ, himself, as the infant born at Christmas, represents the perfection of the *Nous*. As he himself teaches us, "Truly, I say to you, unless you turn and become like children, you will never enter the kingdom of heaven." The infant Christ is the image of the *Nous*, which has become child-like, unattached to worldly things and open to the vision of God.

Finally, the Holy Family is an earthly reflection of the Holy Trinity. Saint Joseph represents God the Father; Mary, the Holy Spirit; Christ, of course, represents Himself. Thus are the powers of the eternal world reflected at every level of being.

Suggestions for practice

Today should be about family, and I invite you to define this as broadly as appropriate. If you have a spouse and children, today you will focus on them. Or you may focus on your siblings and parents, or on whatever group of friends and companions feels like family to you. I've already told you that my own extended family has a tradition of getting together on Saint Stephen's Day. If a like tradition doesn't already exist in your family, today is a great day for it.

Meditation for The Feast of the Holy Family

Today in meditation, consider all that we've said about the Holy Family, both in itself and its earthly mission, and the principle of Justice that is established in it, and as an icon of the Holy Trinity. Consider what these things mean to you, and how you can establish Justice in your own life, both within your soul and in your relationships. And consider the family as an image or icon of the Holy Trinity. What do these things mean to you? How can you establish or expand the principle of Justice in your own life? What does it mean that God manifests to us, first and foremost, as a family?

As you conclude your meditation, you may offer the following prayer:

> To the Holy Family of Jesus, Mary, and Joseph,
> As in all things, you were bound to one another in service of the mission of the Word Incarnate, through the guidance of the Holy Spirit, under the Will of God the Father, may it be that this principle of Justice be established in our hearts and in our homes, today and every day. Through Jesus Christ Our Lord. *Amen.*

CHAPTER THIRTY ONE

New Year's Eve and New Year's Day

Happy New Year!

The first of January has been celebrated as the beginning of the year since the time of Julius Caesar. January, of course, is named for Janus, the god of doorways. Janus has two faces: One looks back into the year now gone by, and the other looks forward into the year to come. *Nomen est omen*, as the saying has it; the names of things are always significant. When the old Pagan world ended, many of its customs and many of its names stuck around. It is our view here that these things never happen by accident—if the name of January endured, then, in a sense, Janus himself endured. In 2,000 years of Christianity no one has succeeded in renaming the months named for Janus, Februros, Mars, Juno, Julius or Augustus, nor the days named for the Sun and Moon, Tyr, Odin, Thor, Frigg and Saturn (or Mars, Mercury, Jupiter, and Venus in Latin countries). That their names endure shows that their power endures, and it must be by the Will of God that this is so; and if it is no longer appropriate to offer sacrifices to them, we can still honor their work in the world in other ways.

Traditional practices

The New Year's Eve Party is probably the best known and best kept of our traditional New Year's observances. The New Year's Eve Party is very old and quite traditional. In earlier times, it was followed by a day of visiting—on New Year's Day, the doors of every house were flung open, and no visitor could be turned away. This custom endured in parts of the United States until well into the 19th century, after which time the refinement of higher proof alcohols led to doors being locked until at least noon on New Year's Day.

Where I was raised in Pennsylvania, it was the custom to eat pork and sauerkraut on New Year's Day, and it was well known that anyone who failed to do so was in for a year of bad luck. This tradition originated with the Germans who settled in most of the state in the 17th and 18th centuries, but it's since spread to many different communities. My grandmother was not the most enthusiastic cook, and so in my home this took the form of canned sauerkraut and spam or hot dogs, which one was still nevertheless required to eat. (In fairness to grandma, she did bring up 13 children, starting in the last days of the Eisenhower Administration and continuing through George W. Bush's second term; at that point, you'd probably open up a can of spam yourself.)

And then there's the New Year's Resolution. This is a very good custom, which traditionally took the form of serious reflection on the year gone by and setting intentions for the year to come. These days, however, it seems mostly to consist of the buying of gym memberships, which are used for two weeks and paid for six months. Any time we participate in a collective activity, we are influenced by the energies of that activity, and the patterns that play out in others tend to play out in us. For this reason, I strongly recommend *avoiding* this kind of New Year's Resolution, as the pattern built up around it is one of abandonment and failure. There is, however, a better way to tap into the renewing energy of the New Year, which I'll come to shortly.

Feast of the Mother of God, Feast of the Circumcision

For many centuries, it was the practice in the Roman Church to observe January 1 as the Feast of the Circumcision, Conferral of the Holy Name of Jesus, and Octave of the Nativity. It is still the Feast of the Circumcision in the Orthodox, Anglican, and Lutheran churches. The Roman Church, in its wisdom, has changed it to the Solemnity of Mary, Mother of God. While I personally support every effort to magnify the devotion given to Our Lady, I dislike the modern Vatican's love of innovation for innovation's sake. Let this day remain the Feast of the Circumcision.

Now, that doesn't make it not a Marian feast as well. Here is the Collect for the day:

> O God, it was through the Motherhood of the Blessed Virgin Mary that You bestowed the gift of eternal life upon mankind. Grant that we may feel the powerful intercession of Mary, through whom we were privileged to receive the giver of life, Jesus Christ, Your Son, Our Lord; who lives and rules with You in the unity of the Holy Spirit, one God forever and ever. *Amen.*

And here is the Gospel:

> At that time, when eight days were fulfilled for the circumcision of the Child, His name was called Jesus, the name given to Him by the Angel before He was conceived in the womb.

We see that these things are united, and we should consider them together in meditation.

New Year's meditation

Rather than simply making a New Year's Resolution which you'll give up two weeks from now and forget all about by Groundhog Day, I recommend an approach to the new year that is at once more general and more intentional. Today, in meditation, take some time to reflect upon the previous year. Go deep and really call it to mind. Ask yourself: What did I learn? How did I grow? What did I achieve? And also ask yourself, How did I fail? How did I fall short of my goals?

Now, ask yourself, who do I want to be a year from now? What virtues do I want to cultivate, and what vices do I need to overcome? How can I grow in holiness? What do I want to achieve and learn?

Take some time to really visualize these things. Imagine yourself a year from now, having grown in virtue, wisdom, and holiness. Who are you, then? Think about these things very generally, and then dial into specifics, and be as detailed as you possibly can.

Finally, a journal is very helpful here. It's critical when we're setting goals for ourselves to *write them down*. Only by doing this can we track our progress. And next year at this time, you will be better able to look back, see where you were at the beginning of 2022, and where you met your goals, where you exceeded them, and where you fell short of them.

You can also break this meditation up a little bit—use New Year's Eve to reflect on the year gone by, and New Year's Day to plan for the year ahead.

Happy New Year!

CHAPTER THIRTY TWO

Eve of Epiphany

January 5 is the Eve of Epiphany, which means the 12 days of Christmas have come to their end.

Tomorrow is the traditional day to bless the home. To do this, in addition to our usual tools, we will use consecrated chalk. Now, if you like, you can bless your chalk tomorrow before you use it, but as it is traditional to bless the chalk on the Eve of the Epiphany, I want to provide the blessing ritual today.

The blessing of Chalk

If you've been following along up to this point, you already know what you need to do. A simple, but complete, system for blessing sacred objects has been provided in these posts, starting from the beginning of Advent. To bless Epiphany Chalk, you'll need your usual implements—at minimum, a quiet place and a table or ledge on which you can place a crucifix, a candle, whatever holy images you find suitable, as well as holy water and incense. And, of course, chalk!

Follow the same procedure given previously to bless incense and wine, but when it comes time to bless the chalk itself, use the following formula. Remember that the "V" and "R" are applicable if you have an assistant; if not, read everything yourself. When you encounter a +, make the Sign of the Cross over the chalk, which you should visualize in the form of white fire.

> V. Our help is in the name of the Lord. R. Who made Heaven and Earth.
> V. The Lord be with you. R. And with Thy Spirit.
>
> Bless, + O Lord God, this creature chalk, to render it helpful to men. Grant that they who use it with faith in Thy most holy Name, and with it inscribe upon the entrance of their homes the names of Thy Saints, Caspar, Melchior, and Balthasar, may through their merits and intercession enjoy health of body and protection of soul. Through Christ Our Lord. R. *Amen.*

Sprinkle the chalk three times with holy water and cense it three times with incense. Your chalk is now ready for your house blessing; we will use it tomorrow.

CHAPTER THIRTY THREE

Epiphany

Happy Epiphany! The Feast of Epiphany commemorates the visitation of the three magi to the infant Jesus; it is the last official day of Christmas—though the Christmas season as a whole goes until Candlemas on February 1.

Traditional observations

There are many old traditions and customs associated with Epiphany, as there have been with the rest of our Feast Days. Many of these have very similar themes; one regularly sees house blessings, various forms of "trick-or-treating," divinations, and the crowning of child-kings and boy-bishops.

Epiphany in particular is associated with cakes in which a small bean or coin is placed; whoever discovers the bean becomes the king of the Epiphany.

Epiphany is also a day for giving gifts. Sometimes the gifts are said to come from the magi; other times, a Santa Claus-type of figure provides them. In Italy and in the Italian diaspora, gifts are distributed by a witch called La Befana; in some households, it's the role of the youngest daughter to put on a witch's hat and pass out presents.

The blessing of the waters is one of the great Epiphany traditions. It is still the custom in many churches to bless natural bodies of water on Epiphany, including lakes, rivers, and the ocean itself. Among the Eastern Orthodox, the ceremony of blessing includes tossing a cross into the water, which the gathered parishioners then compete to find.

It's worth noting that cold water has strong powers of magical purification, which are used in many traditions. You'll find the Greeks at the beginning of the Iliad purifying themselves after offending Apollo by casting themselves into the sea; you'll find modern Japanese Shintoists doing the same sort of thing with waterfalls. Give it a try yourself sometime, if you have a body of water available. You'll find the effects immediate and remarkable—and all the more so if you preface your swim with a suitable prayer.

In Greece, it was also the custom to take ashes from a hearth in which cedarwood had been burning since Christmas to a blessed river, "baptize" the "ashes," and then scatter the ashes at the four corners of vineyards and at the foot of apple and fig trees. Similar customs prevailed as far away as England, where men would drink a toast of cider before the largest apple tree they could find, and sing the following song:

> Here's to thee, old apple-tree,
> Whence thou may'st bud, and whence thou may'st blow!
> And whence thou may'st bear apples enow!
> Hats full! Caps full!
> Bushel!—bushel—sacks full,
> And my pockets full too! Huzza!

Today, the best-known Epiphany devotion is the blessing of the home with water and consecrated chalk. As we discussed yesterday, that's what we're going to do today.

The blessing of the home

Preparation. Begin in the usual way, with the following twist—if you can, you should set up your prayer space either in the kitchen or in some place representing the center of the home to you. For this ritual, you will need consecrated chalk, as described in the last chapter.

Step 1. Perform the usual opening, including the asperges with holy water, censing with incense, and the invocation.

Step 2. Recite the following:

> A. The Prologue to Saint John's Gospel
> B. The Our Father
> C. The Collect:

> O God, who by the star this day revealed Your only-begotten Son to all nations, grant that we, who know You now by faith, may be brought one day before the vision of Your majesty. Through the same Jesus Christ, Our Lord. *Amen.*

Step 3. Now, take your chalk and go outside to the door of your house. At the top part of the door (the lintel), you are going to write the following:

20 + C + M + B + 22

This stands for Caspar, Melchior, and Balthazar, the names of the three magi. And it also stands for *Christus mansionem benedicat*—or Christ bless this house.

Write the formula while reciting the following words:

> The Three Wise Men, Caspar C [write the letter], Melchior M and Balthazar B followed the star of God's Son Who became man, 2,021 years ago. May Christ bless our home ++ [inscribe the first two crosses], and remain with us through the new year ++ [then the last two crosses].

You can then bless the home with holy water. To do this, take your vessel of holy water and make your way through your home. In each room, flick holy water to the four corners of the room, and make the sign of the cross in the center of the room. The water will have an added effect if it is blessed today (or yesterday).

Step 4. Return to the same place you started. Raise your hands and say the following prayer:

> Hear us, holy Lord and Father, almighty everlasting God, and in your goodness send your holy angel from heaven to watch over

and protect all who live in this home, to be with them and give them comfort and encouragement; through Christ Our Lord.

As you do this, visualize an angel descending from Heaven to watch over and protect your home. Know that this is the Guardian Angel of your home and your family as a whole, and that you can turn to him (or her, if it manifests in a feminine form) for help in keeping your home safe and protecting your family from harm or sickness.

Step 5. Close by repeating the asperges and the censing, and add the following prayer:

May thy blessing, Oh Lord, remain upon this home and on those who dwell herein, now and always. *Amen.*

CHAPTER THIRTY FOUR

The Epiphany initiation

Now that we've arrived at the end of our course, I want to offer you something special. This is a ritual of self-initiation into the work of Christian magic.

Remember what we talked about, way back at the beginning of this book. An initiation isn't an ending, it's a beginning. This book has given you the foundation for a Christian magical practice which will serve you well in the years to come.

For this, you will need your altar, which should at least have a crucifix. You will also need a bit of gold, frankincense, and myrrh. Gold, of course, is not very easy to come by in large quantities. Fortunately, it's very easy to find Christmas gift sets with a bits of frankincense and myrrh, as well as gold flecks suspended in water. (If you pick them up this week, you'll get them at a discount.)

Myrrh, gold, and frankincense are the three gifts of the magi, and each has its special meaning. Myrrh was traditionally used to anoint the dead at funerals, and so it stands for Christ's mortal life. The crown of a king is made from gold, and so gold stands for Christ as king of the Jews, and as king of the whole universe. Frankincense, finally, is the traditional incense used in worship, and so it stands for Christ's divinity.

In magical lore, each of these three has additional meanings.

Myrrh is an incense of the planet Saturn. Saturn is slow and cold, related to time and death, and also to the element of Earth. Because Saturn relates to the Earth element, he also signifies the natural world as a whole. As such, Saturn's incense, myrrh, represents natural magic. That is: every form of magic which uses herbs, stones, gems, incense, or other natural materials.

Frankincense is an incense of the Sun, which is the great light of the Heavens; we have already seen that the Sun is a visible icon of the invisible God; in the same way, the visible Heavens of the planets and stars are an icon of the invisible Heaven of the Spiritual World. As such, frankincense stands for all Astral magic. That means every form of magic which relies on the mind, intention, and imagination.

Gold, finally, is a metal which is said to be ruled by both the Sun and Saturn. As it is the metal of kings, it stands for Christ as king of both Heaven (the Sun) and Earth (Saturn). Gold, then, stands for the highest magic, which is nothing more or less than our total devotion to Christ.

In our ritual, we are going to consecrate these three. But we are going to do more than that. Through them, we are going to consecrate every work of natural magic, every work of Astral magic, and our entire devotional life to the Living God.

The ritual

Preparation. Set up your altar in the usual way, and on it place the gold, frankincense, and myrrh.

Step 1. Open with the Banishing Sign of the Cross. Kneel, and say the Our Father, three Hail Marys, and the Glory Be. Then, rise to your feet, and say the invocation:

> Our help is in the Name of the Lord,
> Who hath made the Heavens and the Earth.
> May the Lord be with me and guide my spirit in this work of initiation.

Step 2. Perform the asperges with holy water and the censing with incense.

Step 3. Confess your sins using one of the formulas previously given.

Step 4. Read the following passage from the Gospel of Matthew:

> When Jesus therefore was born in Bethlehem of Judah, in the days of King Herod, behold, there came wise men from the east to Jerusalem.

Saying, Where is he that is born king of the Jews? For we have seen his star in the east, and are come to adore him. And King Herod hearing this, was troubled, and all Jerusalem with him. And assembling together all the chief priests and the scribes of the people, he inquired of them where Christ should be born. But they said to him: In Bethlehem of Judah. For so it is written by the prophet:

And thou Bethlehem the land of Juda art not the least among the princes of Judah: for out of thee shall come forth the captain that shall rule my people Israel. Then Herod, privately calling the wise men, learned diligently of them the time of the star which appeared to them; And sending them into Bethlehem, said: Go and diligently inquire after the child, and when you have found him, bring me word again, that I also may come to adore him. Who having heard the king, went their way; and behold the star which they had seen in the east, went before them, until it came and stood over where the child was. And seeing the star they rejoiced with exceeding great joy.

And entering into the house, they found the child with Mary his mother, and falling down they adored him; and opening their treasures, they offered him gifts; gold, frankincense, and myrrh. And having received an answer in sleep that they should not return to Herod, they went back another way into their country.

Step 5. Take your seat and enter into meditation. Start by visualizing the scene we just read. See the magi, wizards and astrologers, coming from the east to adore the newborn Christ. See them kneel before his crib, with his mother and Saint Joseph beside him. And see them present their gifts.

Step 6. Now, bring to mind the entire work of this course, the customs and traditions, the rituals and meditations. Consider what sort of changes they have wrought in your life. Give thanks to God and offer to Him all of the fruits of this course, and all of the works of magic that you have performed and will perform. Ask for the grace to continue the work you have begun in this course in years to come.

Step 7. Come out of meditation and rise to your feet. Say:

Myrrh, Gold, and Frankincense. Myrrh for his mortal life; gold for his kingship; frankincense for his divinity.

Place the myrrh on the altar.

> Lord, I offer you this gift of myrrh as a sign of my devotion to the Christian Mysteries. Tree of Saturn, gift of the dead, let this gift of myrrh stand for all the works of natural magic, of stones and herbs, roots and water which I may perform now and in times to come. Let them be consecrated to you and ever under your will, this day and always.

Place the frankincense on the altar.

> Lord, I offer you this gift of frankincense as a sign of my devotion to the Christian Mysteries. Fragrance of the Sun, fragrance of prayer, let this gift of frankincense stand for all the works of Astral magic, stars and signs, names and images, which I may perform, now and in times to come. Let them be consecrated to you and ever under your will, this day and always.

Place the gold on the altar.

> Lord, I offer you this gift of gold as a sign of my devotion to the Christian Mysteries. Metal of the Sun, crown of the king, let this gift of gold stand for my entire devotion to you as King of the Universe. Let every prayer and charitable act, every work of thought or word or deed which I may perform, now and in times to come, be consecrated to you and ever under your will, this day and always.
>
> Gold, frankincense, and myrrh. Even as the magi in days of old offered these gifts unto you oh Lord, so do I offer them, and with them, myself, body and soul. May every work of natural magic, every work of Astral magic, all my prayers and every work that I perform in this life be under divine grace and your eternal will. Never allow me to part from you or to fall into works of evil sorcery. Grant that my name may be written in the Book of Life, and guide me in this Earthly pilgrimage, that when I reach the end of the journey I may be united with you forever. Amen.

Step 9. You may wish to sit in contemplation for a time. When you are done, close the ritual in the usual way.

AFTERWORD

The Christian wheel of the year

The work which we have completed in this course is only the beginning. Its purpose is to give you a foundation of practice which you can continue throughout the year and in years to come. Every season has its own traditions and customs, fasts and feasts and devotions. Future volumes in this series will cover the rest of the year, from the day after Epiphany all the way back around to next year's Advent. In the meantime, you are on your own, and I encourage you to do your own research and come up with your own practices, using the work of this book as your foundation.

May God bless you and keep you until we meet again.

APPENDICES

APPENDIX A

A list of commonly used prayers

Here are a number of common prayers, which you may wish to use as part of this course. All of these can be said any time, or they can be prayed as part of your daily practice. Many are suitable as "closing prayers" for the rituals given. Many people like to pray in Latin, and I've included Latin versions of many of the prayers, as well as Latin versions of prayers you most likely know already.

Our Father

> *Our Father*, who art in Heaven, hallowed be thy name. Thy kingdom come, Thy will be done on Earth as it is in Heaven. Give us this day our daily bread, and forgive us our trespasses. [For thine is the kingdom, and the power, and the glory, forever and ever.]

The part in brackets [] is optional; it is said in Anglican and Protestant services, though not usually by Catholics.

> *Pater Noster, qui es in caelis, sanctificetur nomen tuum. Adveniat regnum tuum. Fiat voluntas tua, sicut in caelo et in terra. Panem*

nostrum quotidianum da nobis hodie, et dimitte nobis debita nostra sicut et nos dimittimus debitoribus nostris. Et ne nos inducas in tentationem, sed libera nos a malo. Amen.

Hail Mary

Hail Mary, full of grace, the Lord is with thee. Blessed art thou among women, and blessed is the fruit of thy womb, Jesus. Holy Mary, Mother of God, pray for us sinners, now and at the hour of our death. *Amen.*

Ave Maria, gratia plena, Dominus tecum. Benedicta tu in mulieribus, et benedictus fructus ventris tui, Iesus. Sancta Maria, Mater Dei, ora pro nobis peccatoribus, nunc, et in hora mortis nostrae. Amen.

Glory be

Glory be to the Father, and to the Son, and to the Holy Spirit. As it was in the beginning, is now and forever, unto the ages of ages. Amen.

Gloria Patri, et Filio, et Spiritui Sancto. Sicut erat in principio, et nunc, et semper, et in saecula saeculorum. Amen.

Holy Spirit prayer

Come, Holy Spirit, fill the hearts of thy faithful, and enkindle in them the fire of thy love.

Send forth Thy Spirit and they shall be created, and Thou shalt renew the face of the Earth.

Let us pray: O God, Who didst instruct the hearts of the faithful by the light of the Holy Spirit, grant us in the same Spirit to be truly wise, and ever to rejoice in His consolation, through Christ, Our Lord. Amen.

VENI, Sancte Spiritus, reple tuorum corda fidelium, et tui amoris in eis ignem accende. Emitte Spiritum tuum et creabuntur,t renovabis faciem terrae.

Oremus: DEUS, qui corda fidelium Sancti Spiritus illustratione docuisti. Da nobis in eodem Spiritu recta sapere, et de eius semper consolatione gaudere. Per Christum Dominum nostrum. Amen.

Magnificat in Latin and English

My soul doth magnify the Lord.
And my spirit hath rejoiced in God my Savior.
For he hath regarded: the lowliness of his handmaiden: For behold, from henceforth: all generations shall call me blessed.
For he that is mighty hath magnified me: and holy is his Name.
And his mercy is on them that fear him: throughout all generations.
He hath shewed strength with his arm: he hath scattered the proud in the imagination of their hearts.
He hath put down the mighty from their seat: and hath exalted the humble and meek.
He hath filled the hungry with good things: and the rich he hath sent empty away.
He remembering his mercy hath holpen his servant Israel:
As he promised to our forefathers, Abraham and his seed for ever.

Magnificat anima mea Dominum;
et exultavit spiritus meus in Deo salutari meo,
quia respexit humilitatem ancillae suae;
Ecce enim ex hoc beatam me dicent omnes generationes.
quia fecit mihi magna, qui potens est, et sanctum nomen eius,
Et misericordia eius a progenie in progenies timentibus eum.
Fecit potentiam in brachio suo;
dispersit superbos mente cordis sui;
deposuit potentes de sede, et exaltavit humiles;
esurientes implevit bonis
et divites dimisit inanes.
Suscepit Israel puerum suum, recordatus misericordiae suae,
sicut locutus est ad patres nostros,
Abraham et semini eius in saecula.

Hail, Holy Queen

Hail, Holy Queen, Mother of Mercy,
our life, our sweetness and our hope.
To thee do we cry,
poor banished children of Eve.

To thee do we send up our sighs,
mourning and weeping in this valley of tears.
Turn then, most gracious advocate,
thine eyes of mercy toward us,
and after this our exile
show unto us the blessed fruit of thy womb, Jesus.
O clement, O loving,
O sweet Virgin Mary.

Saint Michael prayer in English and Latin

Saint Michael the Archangel, defend us in battle. Be our protection against the malice and snares of the Devil. May God rebuke him we humbly pray; and do thou, O Prince of the Heavenly host, by the power of God, thrust into Hell Satan and all evil spirits who wander through the world for the ruin of souls. *Amen.*

Sáncte Míchael Archángele, defénde nos in proélio, cóntra nequítiam et insídias diáboli ésto præsídium. Ímperet ílli Déus, súpplices deprecámur: tuque, prínceps milítiæ cæléstis, Sátanam aliósque spíritus malígnos, qui ad perditiónem animárum pervagántur in múndo, divína virtúte, in inférnum detrúde. Ámen.

Guardian Angel prayer

Angel of God, my guardian dear,
To whom God's love commits me here,
Ever this day (night) be at my side,
To light and guard, to rule and guide. Amen.

Fatima prayer

O My Jesus, forgive us our sins, save us from the fires of Hell, lead all souls to Heaven, especially those in most need of Thy mercy.

Prayer of Saint Francis

Lord, make me a channel of thy peace!
That where there is hatred,
I may bring love.

That where there is wrong,
I may bring the spirit of forgiveness.
That where there is discord,
I may bring harmony.
That where there is error,
I may bring truth.
That where there is doubt,
I may bring faith.
That where there is despair,
I may bring hope.
That where there are shadows,
I may bring light.
That where there is sadness,
I may bring joy.
Lord, grant that I may seek rather to comfort,
than to be comforted.
To understand,
than to be understood.
To love,
than to be loved.
For it is by self-forgetting that one finds.
It is by forgiving that one is forgiven.
It is by dying that one awakens to eternal life.

Canticle of the creatures (Song of the Sun)

Most High, all-powerful,
good Lord,
yours is the praise,
the glory and the honor and every blessing.

To you alone, Most High,
do they belong,
and no one is worthy
to speak your name.

Praised be you, my Lord
with all your creatures,
especially Sir Brother Sun,
who is the day through whom
you bring us light.

And he is lovely, shining
with great splendor,
for he heralds you, Most High.

Praised be you, my Lord,
through Sister Moon and Stars.
In heaven you have formed them,
lightsome and precious and fair.

And praised be you, my Lord,
through Brother Wind, through
air and cloud, through calm
and every weather by which
you sustain your creatures.

Praised be you, my Lord,
through Sister Water,
so very useful and humble,
precious and chaste.

Praised be you, my Lord
through Brother Fire,
by whom you light up
the night, and he is
handsome and merry,
robust and strong.

Praised be you, my Lord,
through our Sister, Mother Earth,
who sustains us and directs us
bringing forth all kinds of fruits
and colored flowers and herbs.

Praised be you, my Lord
through those who forgive
for your love
and who bear sickness and trial.

Blessed are those
who endure in peace,
for by you, Most High,
they will be crowned.

Praised be you, my Lord,
through our Sister Bodily Death
from whom no living being
can escape.

How dreadful for those
who die in mortal sin!
How blessed are those she
finds in your most holy will
for the second death
can do them no harm.

O praise and bless my Lord,
thank him and serve him
humbly but grandly!

Creeds and professions of faith

The Nicene Creed

I believe in one God,
the Father almighty,
maker of Heaven and Earth,
of all things visible and invisible.

I believe in one Lord Jesus Christ,
the Only Begotten Son of God,
born of the Father before all ages.
God from God, Light from Light,
true God from true God,
begotten, not made, consubstantial with the Father;
through him all things were made.
For us men and for our salvation
he came down from heaven,

and by the Holy Spirit was incarnate of the Virgin Mary,
and became man.

For our sake he was crucified under Pontius Pilate,
he suffered death and was buried,
and rose again on the third day
in accordance with the Scriptures.

He ascended into heaven
and is seated at the right hand of the Father.
He will come again in glory
to judge the living and the dead
and his kingdom will have no end.

I believe in the Holy Spirit, the Lord, the giver of life,
who proceeds from the Father and the Son,
who with the Father and the Son is adored and glorified,
who has spoken through the prophets.

I believe in one, holy, Catholic and Apostolic Church.
I confess one Baptism for the forgiveness of sins
and I look forward to the resurrection of the dead
and the life of the world to come. Amen.

The confession of faith of Saint Patrick

There is not, nor ever was, any other God—there was none before him and there shall not be any after him—besides him who is God the Father unbegotten: without a source, from him everything else takes its beginning. He is, as we say, the one who keeps hold of all things. And His Son, Jesus Christ, whom we declare to have always existed with the Father.

He was with the Father spiritually before the world came into being; begotten of the Father before the beginning of anything in a way that is beyond our speech. And "through him all things were made," all things visible and invisible. He was made man, and having conquered death was taken back into the Heavens to the Father.

"And he has bestowed on him all power above every name in heaven and on earth and under the earth, so that every tongue may confess that Our Lord and God is Jesus Christ." In him we believe, looking forward to his coming in the very near future when he will judge the living and the dead, and "will repay each according to his works."

And "the Father has plentifully poured upon us the Holy Spirit," the gift and pledge of immortality, who makes those who believe and listen into "sons of God" the Father and "fellow heirs with Christ."

This is whom we profess and worship, One God in Trinity of sacred name. Amen.

The profession of faith of the Liberal Catholic Church

We believe that God is Love and Power and Truth and Light;
that perfect Justice rules the world;
that all His sons shall one day reach His feet, however far they stray.

We hold the Fatherhood of God, the Brotherhood of man,
we know that we do serve Him best
when best we serve our brother man.

So shall His blessing rest on us and peace for evermore.

Amen.

Confiteor prayers

Roman Catholic Confiteor

I confess to Almighty God, to blessed Mary ever Virgin, to blessed Michael the Archangel, to blessed John the Baptist, to the holy apostles Peter and Paul, and to all the saints, that I have sinned exceedingly in thought, word, and deed: through my fault, through my fault, through my most grievous fault. Therefore I beseech blessed Mary ever Virgin, blessed Michael the Archangel, blessed John the Baptist, the holy apostles Peter and Paul, and all the saints, to pray to the Lord our God for me.

May Almighty God have mercy on us,* and, our sins being forgiven, bring us to life everlasting. Amen.

An Anglican prayer of Penitence

Almighty God, our heavenly Father, we have sinned against you and against our neighbor in thought and word and deed, through negligence, through weakness, through our own deliberate fault.

We are truly sorry and repent of all our sins. For the sake of your Son Jesus Christ, who died for us, forgive us all that is past and grant that we may serve you in newness of life to the glory of your name.

Liberal Catholic Confiteor

O Lord, Thou hast created us to be immortal and made us to be an image of Thine own eternity; yet often we forget the glory of our heritage and wander from the path which leads to righteousness. But Thou, O Lord, hast made us for Thyself and our hearts are ever restless till they find their rest in Thee. Look with the eyes of Thy love upon our manifold imperfections and pardon all our shortcomings, that we may be filled with the brightness of the everlasting light and become the unspotted mirror of Thy power and the image of Thy goodness; through Christ Our Lord. Amen.

May God the Father, God the Son, God the Holy Spirit, bless, preserve and sanctify us; may the Lord in his loving kindness look down upon us and be gracious unto us; may the Lord absolve me from all our sins and grant unto us the grace and comfort of the Holy Spirit. Amen.

*In each of these versions of the Confiteor, I'm preserving the first-person plural form from the Mass, in order to remind us of the fact that we are never alone in this journey. If it feels more appropriate to you to use the first-person singular—that is, "I," "me," in place of "we," "us"—please do so.

The Rosary

The Rosary is a very big topic, and to do it justice would require a book in itself! In fact, many such books have already been written by authors far more qualified than I (some of these are mentioned further down). That said, it would be negligent to write a book on the magical side of Christianity without at least mentioning the Rosary, one of the very greatest devotionals of the Catholic Church.

You may include the Rosary as part of your daily devotion or as a substitute for the system of meditation presented here. The Rosary is a set of prayer beads, ending in a crucifix, and often including a saint's medal. The Rosary is divided into a set of three small beads, then five sets of ten beads. The ten beads are divided by one larger bead. Each of the sets of ten is associated with one of 15 mysteries. These mysteries are events from the lives of Jesus and Mary. The mysteries are divided into sets of five, called the Joyful, Sorrowful, and Glorious Mysteries. Again, if you wish to explore the Rosary, there are many resources available to you. But if you have never worked with it before or simply need a refresher, here is a basic guide.

Step 1. Begin by saying the Our Father and a confession of faith of your choice (the Apostle's Creed is most common).

Step 2. At the three small beads above the crucifix, pray one Hail Mary each.

Step 3. Now, announce the first mystery to be prayed (see below), which is an event from the life of Our Lord and His Blessed Mother. Quiet your mind, and enter into meditation on the mystery for a brief time.

Step 4. When you feel ready, say the Our Father, and one Hail Mary for each of the ten small beads. Close with the Glory Be. While you pray, try to keep your mind focused on the words of the prayer while holding the sense or feeling of the mystery in your mind.

Step 5. At the end of all five mysteries, close with the Hail Holy Queen. You may also wish to say the Saint Michael Prayer.

List of the Mysteries

Joyful Mysteries: Monday and Thursday

1. The Annunciation
2. The Visitation
3. The Birth of Our Lord
4. The Coming of the Magi
5. The Finding of Our Lord in the Temple

Sorrowful Mysteries: Tuesday and Friday

1. The Agony in the Garden
2. The Scourging at the Pillar
3. The Crown of Thorns
4. Jesus Carries His Cross
5. Jesus Dies on the Cross and is Buried

APPENDIX A

Glorious Mysteries

1. Jesus rises from the Dead
2. Jesus ascends into Heaven
3. The Holy Spirit descends at Pentecost
4. The Assumption of Our Lady
5. Our Lady is Crowned Queen of Heaven and Earth

APPENDIX B

Making your own holy water

There are a great many sacramentals beyond those few covered in this book; so many, indeed, that it would take another long book to cover them all. If you're interested in working more extensively in the sacramentals, *The Book of Sacramental Magic* covers them in great detail. The best known, and most versatile, of all the sacramentals is holy water. Holy water has a multitude of uses, including spiritual protection, preparation of the soul for prayer and initiation. You can sprinkle it in your home or your car to bring health and protection, or sprinkle it on a cross or other sacred object as a minor blessing. You can easily find holy water at a Catholic or Orthodox church, but you can also make it yourself. Modern Catholic churches usually use a new rite, introduced in the 1960s, to bless holy water, and in my experience, it just isn't as effective. The complete old rite for blessing holy water is included below. You can use it as is or in combination with the ritual formula given in this book. Please note: Whenever you come across a "+" in the text that follows, trace the sign of the cross over the salt or water as indicated. You should visualize the cross in the form of blazing white light.

Ritual for holy water:

> Our help is in the name of the Lord.
> Who made Heaven and Earth.

The exorcism of salt follows:

> God's creature, salt, I cast out the demon from you by the living + God, by the true + God, by the holy + God, by God who ordered you to be thrown into the water-spring by Eliseus to heal it of its barrenness. May you be a purified salt, a means of health for those who believe, a medicine for body and soul for all who make use of you. May all evil fancies of the foul fiend, his malice and cunning, be driven afar from the place where you are sprinkled. And let every unclean spirit be repulsed by Him who is coming to judge both the living and the dead and the world by fire.
> *Amen.*

Let us pray.

> Almighty everlasting God, we humbly appeal to your mercy and goodness to graciously bless + this creature, salt, which you have given for mankind's use. May all who use it find in it a remedy for body and mind. And may everything that it touches or sprinkles be freed from uncleanness and any influence of the evil spirit; through Christ Our Lord.
> *Amen.*

Exorcism of the water:

> God's creature, water, I cast out the demon from you in the name of God + the Father almighty, in the name of Jesus + Christ, His Son, Our Lord, and in the power of the Holy + Spirit. May you be a purified water, empowered to drive afar all power of the enemy, in fact, to root out and banish the enemy himself, along with his fallen angels. We ask this through the power of Our Lord Jesus Christ, who is coming to judge both the living and the dead and the world by fire.
> *Amen.*

Let us pray.

> O God, who for man's welfare established the most wonderful mysteries in the substance of water, hearken to our prayer, and pour forth your blessing + on this element now being prepared with various purifying rites. May this creature of yours, when used in your mysteries and endowed with your grace, serve to cast out demons and to banish disease. May everything that this water sprinkles in the homes and gatherings of the faithful be delivered from all that is unclean and hurtful; let no breath of contagion hover there, no taint of corruption; let all the wiles of the lurking enemy come to nothing. By the sprinkling of this water may everything opposed to the safety and peace of the occupants of these homes be banished, so that in calling on your holy name they may know the well-being they desire, and be protected from every peril; through Christ Our Lord.
> *Amen.*

Pour the salt into the water, and say:

> May this salt and water be mixed together; in the name of the Father, and of the Son, + and of the Holy Spirit.
> *Amen.*
>
> The Lord be with you.
> May He also be with you.

Let us pray.

> God, source of irresistible might and king of an invincible realm, the ever-glorious conqueror; who restrain the force of the adversary, silencing the uproar of his rage, and valiantly subduing his wickedness; in awe and humility we beg you, Lord, to regard with favor this creature thing of salt and water, to let the light of your kindness shine upon it, and to hallow it with the dew of your mercy; so that wherever it is sprinkled and your holy name is invoked, every assault of the unclean spirit may be baffled, and all dread of the serpent's venom be cast out. To us who entreat your mercy, grant that the Holy Spirit may be with us wherever we may be; through Christ Our Lord.
> *Amen.*

APPENDIX C

Psalms and their magical uses

Psalm 5

The Psalm 5 is traditionally used for protection against liars; for the souls of the dead; to save a city under siege; and to obtain the friendship of lords or powerful people.

> Give ear to my words, O Lord, consider my meditation.
> Hearken unto the voice of my cry, my King, and my God: for unto thee will I pray.
> My voice shalt thou hear in the morning, O Lord; in the morning will I direct my prayer unto thee, and will look up.
> For thou art not a God that hath pleasure in wickedness: neither shall evil dwell with thee.
> The foolish shall not stand in thy sight: thou hatest all workers of iniquity.
> Thou shalt destroy them that speak leasing: the Lord will abhor the bloody and deceitful man.
> But as for me, I will come into thy house in the multitude of thy mercy: and in thy fear will I worship toward thy holy temple.

> Lead me, O Lord, in thy righteousness because of mine enemies; make thy way straight before my face.
> For there is no faithfulness in their mouth; their inward part is very wickedness; their throat is an open sepulchre; they flatter with their tongue.
> Destroy thou them, O God; let them fall by their own counsels; cast them out in the multitude of their transgressions; for they have rebelled against thee.
> But let all those that put their trust in thee rejoice: let them ever shout for joy, because thou defendest them: let them also that love thy name be joyful in thee.
> For thou, Lord, wilt bless the righteous; with favour wilt thou compass him as with a shield.

Psalm 23

The Psalm 23 (which is the Psalm 22 in Catholic Bibles) is especially used for protection during travel. It is also used for spiritual protection generally, and to obtain honors.

> The Lord is my shepherd; I shall not want.
> He maketh me to lie down in green pastures: he leadeth me beside the still waters.
> He restoreth my soul: he leadeth me in the paths of righteousness for his name's sake.
> Yea, though I walk through the valley of the shadow of death, I will fear no evil: for thou art with me; thy rod and thy staff they comfort me.
> Thou preparest a table before me in the presence of mine enemies: thou anointest my head with oil; my cup runneth over.
> Surely goodness and mercy shall follow me all the days of my life: and I will dwell in the house of the Lord for ever.

Psalm 46

The Psalm 46 is traditionally used for protection by those going into combat; in practice, it will help with any stressful, dangerous, or competitive situation. Amusingly, it was also used by husbands to calm the anger of their wives!

> God is our refuge and strength, a very present help in trouble.
>
> Therefore will not we fear, though the earth be removed, and though the mountains be carried into the midst of the sea.
>
> Though the waters thereof roar and be troubled, though the mountains shake with the swelling thereof. Selah.
>
> There is a river, the streams whereof shall make glad the city of God, the holy place of the tabernacles of the most High.
>
> God is in the midst of her; she shall not be moved: God shall help her, and that right early.
>
> The heathen raged, the kingdoms were moved: he uttered his voice, the earth melted.
>
> The Lord of hosts is with us; the God of Jacob is our refuge. Selah.
>
> Come, behold the works of the Lord, what desolations he hath made in the earth.
>
> He maketh wars to cease unto the end of the earth; he breaketh the bow, and cutteth the spear in sunder; he burneth the chariot in the fire.
>
> Be still, and know that I am God: I will be exalted among the heathen, I will be exalted in the earth.
>
> The Lord of hosts is with us; the God of Jacob is our refuge. Selah.

Psalm 136

Psalm 136 (Psalm 135 in Catholic Bibles) is traditionally used to overcome one's enemies. In practice, it should not be used to defeat or cause harm to another, but rather to strengthen your own spirits in any situation of adversity.

> O give thanks unto the Lord; for he is good: for his mercy endureth for ever.
>
> O give thanks unto the God of gods: for his mercy endureth for ever.
>
> O give thanks to the Lord of lords: for his mercy endureth for ever.
>
> To him who alone doeth great wonders: for his mercy endureth for ever.
>
> To him that by wisdom made the Heavens: for his mercy endureth for ever.

To him that stretched out the earth above the waters: for his mercy endureth for ever.
To him that made great lights: for his mercy endureth for ever:
The sun to rule by day: for his mercy endureth for ever:
The moon and stars to rule by night: for his mercy endureth for ever.
To him that smote Egypt in their firstborn: for his mercy endureth for ever:
And brought out Israel from among them: for his mercy endureth for ever:
With a strong hand, and with a stretched out arm: for his mercy endureth for ever.
To him which divided the Red sea into parts: for his mercy endureth for ever:
And made Israel to pass through the midst of it: for his mercy endureth for ever:
But overthrew Pharaoh and his host in the Red sea: for his mercy endureth for ever.
To him which led his people through the wilderness: for his mercy endureth for ever.
To him which smote great kings: for his mercy endureth for ever:
And slew famous kings: for his mercy endureth for ever:
Sihon king of the Amorites: for his mercy endureth for ever:
And Og the king of Bashan: for his mercy endureth for ever:
And gave their land for an heritage: for his mercy endureth for ever:
Even an heritage unto Israel his servant: for his mercy endureth for ever.
Who remembered us in our low estate: for his mercy endureth for ever:
And hath redeemed us from our enemies: for his mercy endureth for ever.
Who giveth food to all flesh: for his mercy endureth for ever.
O give thanks unto the God of heaven: for his mercy endureth for ever.

APPENDIX D

A brief guide to incense

This course suggests the use of incense, and provides methods for blessing incense and for using it to bless your home and working space. Now, many people these days are either unfamiliar with the use of incense or react poorly to it. In either case, the result tends to be some fear around its use. Now, let me be clear: *You are not required to use incense if you do not want to*. If it bothers you or if you have a health condition which makes the use of incense impossible, you can get by perfectly well without it. That said, many people would like to use incense but simply don't know how, and it is for them that this brief guide is intended.

In this guide, I want to present two things. First, we'll talk about several different ways to make use of incense, presenting various options so you can figure out which one works best for you. Second, I'm going to present a guide to the traditional magical uses for various incense plants first, several ways to make use of incense, in order to

The use of incense

Incense can be divided into three types: resin incense, stick incense, and natural incense.

Resin incense is the most commonly used in churches; it is also the most difficult to use at home. As the name implies, resin incense consists of the resin of certain trees, especially frankincense, myrrh, and benzoin.

In order to use resin incense, you're going to need a few different tools. First, you'll need an incense burner. These can be purchased online or at a Catholic supply store. Next, you're going to need some self-lighting charcoal and a pair of tongs to hold onto it.

This is the part where many people go wrong. Self-lighting charcoal is very helpful. The basic procedure is to take a flame to it and allow it to heat up, then set it in your incense burner and place the loose resin onto it. The trouble is: on its own, self-lighting charcoal stinks. For the first few minutes after you light it, it will emit an acrid smoke which I personally find very unpleasant and which many people will find unbearable, especially if you're suffering from asthma or a chest cold.

Fortunately, there is a solution: Simply light the charcoal and place it in its incense burner outside. Leave it alone for a few minutes. After a little while, it will stop smoking, but it will be hot. You can then add resin to it—frankincense, benzoin, or whatever you have—and you will get the smell of the incense without the acrid charcoal stench.

Now, many people still have a hard time with resin incense, and some have allergies to frankincense in particular. That brings us to our next option.

Stick incense comes in a couple of different forms. At malls across America you can buy incense in little boxes with labels like "frankincense and myrrh" or "rose" or "Spring Rain." The incense consists of resins and, often, artificial fragrances, glued to a bamboo core. In my experience, these are just as unpleasant as self-lighting charcoal. I recommend avoiding them entirely.

Fortunately, there is another sort of stick incense. These are sticks of resins held together by natural adhesives without a bamboo stick in the middle. The very best are those which come from Japan or Korea. The ingredients are entirely natural, and usually consist of fragrances which have strong magical properties. My personal favorite is a blend called "Moss Garden" by the Japanese company Shoyeido, which is distributed in the United States. The herbs in this incense include sandalwood, patchouli, and benzoin, all of which are conducive to a meditative state.

Still, even this may be too much for some people. That brings us to our third option.

Natural incense consists of actual plants. In my experience, natural incenses have three great advantages. In the first case, with the exception of sage, they don't stay lit for very long, so it's easy to control the amount of smoke. In the second case, their scent is often no stronger than that of a campfire, and many people who can't handle any sort of resin can tolerate them. And in the third case, natural incense is something that you can make all by yourself. All you need to do is find the plant in question, cut a small amount of it, and allow it to dry.

If you do this, you should talk to the plant, tell it your purpose and why you want to harvest a part of it. It's always polite to pour out a gift of water in return. If at any time you get the sense that you shouldn't do this or the plant doesn't want to participate, back off and find a different plant. Refer back to the chapter on harvesting a Christmas tree for more.

A list of common incense plants and their magical properties

Benzoin—Benzoin purifies the energetic environment, drives off hostile spirits and counters evil magic. Associated with the Sun.

Camphor—Camphor is associated with the Moon; it can be used to invoke lunar energies.

Cedar—Cedar is a powerful protective tree. Simply growing it on a property can help keep negative influences away. When dried, its needles produce a pleasantly scented smoke. Cedar incense has been in use for centuries, if not millennia, on both sides of the Atlantic. It has the ability to drive off evil spirits, negative energies and hostile magic, and creates a sense of devotion. Please note: The trees which are called "cedar" in North America, such as Western Red Cedar—commonly used as a landscaping plant—and Incense Cedar, are not true cedars but cypresses. Nevertheless, they have the same properties as true cedar and were used for the same purposes.

Juniper—The uses of juniper are identical to those of cedar.

Frankincense—Frankincense is the most common traditional incense. One of the gifts of the magi, frankincense, has the special power of elevating the mind toward spiritual things. C.W. Leadbeater writes that "Frankincense vibrates at the frequency of devotion."

Mugwort—Mugwort is another common plant, easy to find in the woods of North America from California to the East Coast. It is traditionally a dream herb, used to bring on psychic states and lucid dreaming. In a blend, it can be combined with a protective herb such as rosemary to create an incense that at once clears the Astral air and opens up the psychic faculties. Mugwort is associated with Mercury.

Myrrh—Myrrh is another traditional gift of the magi. Associated with Saturn, the cold, slow planet of time, death, and restriction, its uses are similar to benzoin, but the feeling it creates is subtly different. Where benzoin purifies the energetic space, myrrh also creates a heavy, serious and even funereal quality. Best used on solemn occasions.

Rosemary—Rosemary is a common herb, used as a landscaping plant in warm climates, with powerful magical properties. Burned as an incense, it is similar to frankincense, both protective and elevating. A sprig of it can also be brushed along the body a few inches from the skin to act as a kind of "lint roller" for the aura! Rosemary is associated with both the Sun and the Moon in various traditions.

Palo santo—Palo santo is a South American relative of frankincense. It has much the same effects as frankincense itself. You won't find it growing wild in North America, but these days Palo santo sticks can be purchased at metaphysical stores, gift shops and cafes all over the United States. It has the great advantage that, being a natural wood, it's much easier for many people to tolerate than pure frankincense resin.

Patchouli—Patchouli is a common traditional incense herb. It is musty and earthy, associated with the element of Earth. In my experience, it is best used as part of a blend, as it adds an element of calm and grounding.

Rose—Rose is the flower of love. As incense, its scent is as sweet as the flower itself. It can be used to produce feelings of romantic love, and also to connect with the higher form of love, which is called agape in the Christian tradition: the selfless love of God and neighbor, which is the Great Commandment of Our Lord.

Sage—Sage may be the best-known protective incense these days, as "saging" has become a part of popular culture. If you ever watch those paranormal shows on TV, the "ghost hunters" will often advise their clients to burn sage to clear out ghosts or negative energies. It does indeed do this, but, unlike most natural incenses, on its own it produces an enormous amount of smoke, and you may not like the scent of it (I don't).

Sandalwood—Sandalwood is a traditional meditation incense throughout much of Asia. You will find many meditation blends include it, and you can use it for this purpose as well. It calms the mind and elevates it toward higher things. Astrologically, it is associated with Venus.

Fir, **spruce**, and **pine** are all useful as incense as well. There isn't a lot of detailed lore on them, but they seem to have the same sorts of properties as cedar—they clear the air of negative influences and conduce to a meditative state.

APPENDIX E

Correspondences of the tradition planets and the four elements

Saturn. Saturn rules sorrow, time, age, death, limitation and confinement, and also rules philosophy. His colors are black and deep purple. The archangel of Saturn is named Cassiel, and the Divine Name which governs Saturn is Elohim. Saturday is the day of Saturn.

Jupiter. Jupiter rules joy, growth and expansion, wealth, and religion. His color is indigo. The archangel of Jupiter is named Zadkiel, and the Divine Name that governs Jupiter is Yahweh Elohim. Thursday is the day of Jupiter.

Mars. Mars rules men, fire, conflict and struggle of all kinds, athletic contests, and also animal husbandry. His color is red. The archangel of Mars is named Kamael and the Divine Name that governs Mars is Elohim Gebur. Tuesday is the day of Mars.

Sun. The Sun rules health, good fortune, power and vitality. His colors are white and gold. The archangel of the Sun is named Michael, and the Divine Name that governs the Sun is Yahweh Eloah Ve'Da'ath. Sunday is the day of the Sun.

Venus. Venus rules women, love, beauty, and sexuality. Her colors are green and rose. The archangel of Venus is named Hanael, and the Divine Name governing Venus is Yahweh Tzava'oth. Friday is the Day of Venus.

Mercury. Mercury rules travel, communication, the marketplace, magic, trickery and illusion. The archangel of Mercury is named Raphael, and the Divine Name governing Mercury is Elohim Tzava'oth. Wednesday is the day of Mercury.

Moon. The Moon rules the home and the common people, mothers and childbirth, and everything to do with water. The archangel of the Moon is named Gabriel, and the Divine Name governing the Moon is Gabriel. Monday is the day of the Moon.

Air. Air is Hot and Moist. The element of Air rules the East, the Spring, morning, youth, and beginnings generally. The archangel of Air is Raphael.

Fire. Fire is Hot and Dry. The element of Fire rules the South, the Summer, noon, maturity, and things reaching their culmination. The archangel of Fire is Michael.

Water. Water is Cold and Moist. The element of Water rules the West, the Autumn, evening, middle age, and the harvest, whether literally or metaphorically. The archangel of Water is Gabriel.

Earth. Earth is Cold and Dry. The element of Earth rules the North, the Winter, nighttime, old age, and the end of things. The archangel of Earth is Uriel.

APPENDIX F

Additional resources

Readers who have enjoyed this book may find the following volumes on Christian esotericism and tradition helpful.

The Magic of Catholicism, by Brother A.D.A.

A must-have for any serious practitioner, this book is many ways, this book is the last word in magical Catholicism. Available along with many other books in the same vein at thauvmapub.com.

The Experience of the Inner Worlds, by Gareth Knight

Knight was at once a devout Anglican and an Esotericist in the tradition of Dion Fortune, and this book provides a gentle and effective introduction to the traditions of Christian magic.

The Red Church, by Christopher Bilardi

This book explores the tradition of braucherei, which is the traditional system of magic of the Pennsylvania Germans. As the author makes clear from the beginning, this is an entirely Christian system of magic, though many of the practices may seem quite strange to the modern reader.

Rituale Romanum

The Rituale is the Catholic Church's official book of rites for both the sacraments and sacramentals. If you can read Latin, you can find very old editions on websites like archive.org. St Cyprian's Press has also released a complete translation in formal, Elizabethan English, rather than the pedestrian English of modern translations. It is available online at https://www.lulu.com/shop/editors-of-saint-cyprian-press/the-roman-ritual-the-blessings-processions-litanies/paperback/product-149r9qgz.html.

Christmas in Ritual and Tradition by Clement A. Miles

Written in 1912, this book is a treasure trove of old customs, traditions, and lore. Best of all, since it's long out of print you can find it online for free.

The Christmas Book by Francis X. Weiser

Written in 1954, this is a fine old book, exploring Christmas traditions and rituals from around the world.

Rosicrucian Cosmo-Conception, by Max Heindel

Written in 1925, this is a very different sort of book, at once deeply devout and totally radical. The Rosicrucian tradition approaches Christianity through the lens of the Esoteric tradition, especially as formulated in the 19th and early 20th centuries.

The Book of Gold

This is a 17th-century collection of magical formulas based on the Psalms and is the source for the Psalm magic in this book. Recently translated by David Rankin and Paul Harry Barron.

APPENDIX G

Calendars for Agent and Christmas for 2025–2035

2025

First Sunday: November 30
Second Sunday: December 7
Third Sunday: December 14
Fourth Sunday: December 21
Christmas falls on a Thursday this year.

2026

First Sunday: November 29
Second Sunday: December 6
Third Sunday: December 13
Fourth Sunday: December 20
Christmas falls on a Friday this year.

2027

First Sunday: November 28
Second Sunday: December 5

Third Sunday: December 12
Fourth Sunday: December 19
Christmas falls on a Saturday this year.

2028

First Sunday: December 3
Second Sunday: December 10
Third Sunday: December 17
Fourth Sunday: December 24
Christmas falls on a Monday this year.

2029

First Sunday: December 2
Second Sunday: December 9
Third Sunday: December 16
Fourth Sunday: December 23
Christmas falls on a Tuesday this year.

2030

First Sunday: December 1
Second Sunday: December 8
Third Sunday: December 15
Fourth Sunday: December 22
Christmas falls on a Wednesday this year.

2031

First Sunday: November 30
Second Sunday: December 7
Third Sunday: December 14
Fourth Sunday: December 21
Christmas falls on a Thursday this year.

2032

First Sunday: November 28
Second Sunday: December 5

Third Sunday: December 12
Fourth Sunday: December 19
Christmas falls on a Saturday this year.

2033

First Sunday: November 27
Second Sunday: December 4
Third Sunday: December 11
Fourth Sunday: December 18
Christmas falls on a Sunday this year.

2034

First Sunday: December 3
Second Sunday: December 10
Third Sunday: December 17
Fourth Sunday: December 24
Christmas falls on a Monday this year.

2035

First Sunday: December 2
Second Sunday: December 9
Third Sunday: December 16
Fourth Sunday: December 23
Christmas falls on a Tuesday this year.

APPENDIX H

Notes

Page 2 – The definition of myth comes from Sallust, *On the Gods and the World*. Translated by Murray, Gilbert. Accessed online at https://hermetic.com/texts/on_the_gods-1.

Page 38 – CS Lewis, Letter to J.R.R. Tolkien. Accessed online at https://judithwolfe.wp.st-andrews.ac.uk/files/2017/08/Letters-to-Arthur-Greeves-1931.pdf.

Page 58 – Geogallis, Julia. *How to Eat Your Christmas Tree: Delicious, Innovative Recipes for Cooking with Trees*. London, Hardy Grant Books. 2020.

Page 62 – Weiss, Sonja. "Turning to God: Some Aspects of the Neoplatonic Conversion." 2023.

Page 63 – The discussion of the two currents of magical power comes from Greer, John Michael. *The Druid Magic Handbook*. Newburyport, MA, Red Wheel/Weiser, LLC. 2007.

Page 70 – This and all citations from this book are from Miles, Clement. *Christmas in Ritual and Tradition*. Out of print, accessed online at https://sacred-texts.com/time/crt/index.htm.

APPENDIX H

Page 82 – Plato, *Republic*. Shorey, Paul, translator. In Hamilton, Edith and Cairns, Huntington, *Plato: Collected Dialogues*. Princeton, NJ, Princeton University Press. 1973.

Page 82 – The discussion of the three parts of the soul is indebted to a talk on Orthodox Anthropology, found online at: https://www.ancientfaith.com/specials/orthodox_anthropology/. Currently unavailable.

Page 95 – The quotation from *Albion's Seed* is from Fischer, David Hackett. *Albion's Seed: Four British Folkways in America*. New York, NY, Oxford University Press. 1989.

Page 97 – The quotation from Jacopo de Voragine is from *The Golden Legend*. Found online at https://www.fisheaters.com/emberdays.html.

Page 114 – The quotation from Gospel of Thomas is saying number 22, translated by Lambdin, Thomas O. Accessed online at https://www.marquette.edu/maqom/Gospel%20of%20Thomas%20Lambdin.pdf.

Page 120 – The quotation from Dionysius is from the translation by Parker, John. The Works of Dionysius the Areopagite. London, James Parker and Co., 1897.

Page 166 – The discussion of Christian marriage comes from Chrysostom, John, *On Marriage and Family Life. Popular Patristics Series*. Delhi, Grapevine India Publishers. 2024.

Page 154 – The blessing of wine is derived in part from the *Rituale Romanum*. Available online at https://www.ewtn.com/catholicism/library/roman-ritual-part-2-11883.

Page 159 – The Childermas prayer is traditional.

Page 162 – Thomas Pinchbeck, *Breaking Open the Head*. New York, Broadway Books. 2003.

Page 174 – The Blessing of Chalk is also from the *Rituale Romanum*.

Page 203 – The magical uses from the psalms come from Rankine, David and Barron, Paul Henry, translators. *The Book of Gold*. London, Avalonia Books. 2010.

Page 213 – Much of the material on the magical use of plants is derived from Greer, John Michael. *Natural Magic: Potions and Powers from the Magical Garden*. Llewelyn Publications, Saint Paul, MN, 2000.

ACKNOWLEDGEMENTS

Like the previous book in this series, this one could not have been written without a great deal of help. Again, I'd like to first thank my wife, for her constant support, and my children, who were test subjects for much of the material in this book.

I'd also like to thank the many readers who read this material when it was a series of disjointed blog posts in an out of the way corner of the internet. Your enthusiasm for this project has been my greatest source of motivation.

I'd again like to thank the team at Aeon books, for making it possible to bring this work to a larger audience.

Finally, the saints of Christmas, Thomas, Andrew, Nicholas and Lucy; Stephen, John, Thomas, the Innocents and the Magi; and above all, the Incarnate Christ and the Blessed Mother, have guided this work from its beginning. *Deo gratias.*

INDEX

Acts of the Apostles, 149–150, 152
Advent, 7, 137
    candles, 29–30
    first Sunday in, 27–28
    fourth Sunday in, 109–111
    Fridays in, 83–84
    material culture of devotion, 8–9
    and Second Coming, 31–37
    second Sunday in, 63–65
    third Sunday in. *See* Gaudete Sunday
Advent Wreath, 9, 29
    blessing for, 21–23
    candle symbolism, 29–30
    colors, 20
    first candle, 28, 29
    fourth candle, 110–111
    second candle, 65
    symbolism and practice, 20–21
    third candle, 91
"aeviternal", 33
Saint Agatha, 94
Air, 214

Albion's Seed (Fischer), 96
alchemist, 51
Alchemy, 51
almsgiving, 81–82
    Fridays in Advent, 83–84
    magical uses of, 84–85
    path of repentance, 82
    psychic anatomy, 82
    as spiritual practice, 85
    tripartite soul, 82
amulets. *See* sacramentals
Saint Andrew, xxix, 43–44
    Saint Andrew's Day, 43–47
    Christmas Novena, 45, 46–47
    Eve, 44–45
    traditions and practices, 44–46
angels, xxvii–xxviii
    Guardian Angel, 39–41, 190
    magic, 39
An Anglican prayer of Penitence, 195
anicca, 34
Saint Anna, 76
annunciation, 144–146

apocalypse, unpredictable, 35
apostles, the, 58, 96, 195
Apostolic Johannite Church, 153
appetite, 12
Aquinas, Thomas, xxvi
archangels, xxviii
    elemental, 100
    Michael, xxxv, 190
    of planets, 213–214
    Saint Raphael the Archangel, 84
    Uriel, 51
Aristotle, 65, 166
Arius, 68
Astral Plane, xxxi–xxxiii, 36, 103.
        See also Law of the Planes
astrology, xxxii
Saint Augustine, 76
aura, 56

banishing ritual, 56
Baptism, infant, 76. *See also* Original Sin
Barron, P. H., 216
Beatific Vision, 76
benzoin, 209
Bethlehem Candle, 65
Bible, 9, 29
    bibliomancy, 96
    as myth, 32
    Psalms, 9, 29, 203–206
    stories, 135
Bilardi, C., 215–216
Saint Blaise, xxix
Blavatsky, Madame, 56
Blessed Virgin Mary, xxx–xxxi, 145, 166, 167
    Hail Mary prayer, 188
The Book of Gold, 216
"Breaking Open the Head", 162–163
Brother A.D.A., 215
Buddha, Gautama, 12

Caesar, 135
Calvinist Churches, 140
camphor, 209
candle, 29–30
    Bethlehem Candle, 65
    first candle, 28, 29
    fourth candle, 110–111
    second candle, 64, 65
    third candle, 91
Canticle of the creatures (Song of the Sun), 191–193
cave, 147
cedar, 209
census, 135, 147
change, 34
charity, 19
    Advent Wreath, 20–23
    Gospel of Luke, 20
Cherubim, xxvii, xxviii
Childermas, 157
    practices, 158
    prayer and meditation, 159
    in tradition, 158
Christianity
    Christ as history and myth, 33
    Christian Astrology, 83–84
    myth and tradition, 32
    traditional, xiii
Christian liturgical cycle. *See* "Christian Wheel of the Year"
Christian magic foundations, 55, 81
    almsgiving, 81–85
    consecrating sacramentals, 123–127
    forgiveness, 103–105
"Christian Wheel of the Year", xiii, 183
The Christmas Book (Weiser), 216
Christmas calendars 2025–2035, 217–219
Christmas Day, 137
    annunciation, 144–146
    creation, 140–141
    descent of human soul, 142–143
    genealogy, 143–144
    incarnation, 146–147
    meaning of Christmas, 139–140
    meditation, 138–139
    practice, 137–138
Christmas Eve, 133
    fasting, 133–134
    reading from Holy Gospel, 134–136

Christmas in Ritual and Tradition (Miles), 70, 115, 150, 216
Christmas Tree, 49
   Alchemy of Christmas preparation, 51
   blessing ceremony, 52–53
   choosing and harvesting, 50–51
   real *vs.* artificial trees, 50
   sustainable and sacred uses, 53–54
   symbolism and spiritual meaning, 49–50
Collective Karma, 77–78. *See also* Original Sin
The confession of faith of Saint Patrick, 194–195
Confiteor prayers, 195
creation, 140–141
creeds and professions of faith, 193
   The confession of faith of Saint Patrick, 194–195
   The Nicene Creed, 193–194
   The profession of faith of the Liberal Catholic Church, 195
Cyprian, 55

death, 143
demons, 78
descent of human soul, 142–143
devil, xxxiv
Diocletian, Emperor, 93–94
Dion Fortune, xv, xvi
Dionysius the Areopagite, xxvi, xxvii, 120
divination, 96
Divine Mind, 141
divine plane. *See* plane of unity
divine power, movements, 57–58
dukkha, 34
Saint Dymphna, xxix

Earth, 214
elemental archangels, 100
Ember Days, 97, 120–121
   element of Earth, 100
   fasting, 100–101
   prayer and meditation, 101–102

   Sacred Cycles of the Year, 97–99
   Winter Ember Days, 100
Energetic Plane, xxxiii–xxxiv. *See also* Law of the Planes
Epiphany, 131, 175
   blessing of home, 176–178
   blessing of waters, 176
   Chalk, 173
   Eve of, 173–174
   traditions and customs, 175–176
Epiphany initiation, 179
   frankincense, 179, 180
   gifts of Magi, 179–180
   gold, 179, 180
   myrrh, 179–180
   ritual, 180–182
Esoteric Christianity
   Immaculate Conception, 78–79
   Original Sin, 77–78
"esotericism", xviii
Esoteric tradition, xviii–xix
Eternal Man, 141
eternity, 32
   and aeviternity, 32–33
   and Intellectual Plane, 35–36
Eve of Epiphany, 173
   blessing of Chalk, 173–174
"evil eye", 103
evil spirits, xxxiv
exorcism
   of salt, 200
   of water, 200–201
The Experience of the Inner Worlds (Knight), 215

fasting, 11
   appetite, 12
   extra days, 14
   purposes, 11–12
   and second fall, 11–13
   second fall, 12–13
   sub-natural condition, 12–13
   three levels of, 13–14
Fatima prayer, 190
Feast of the Circumcision, 170–171
Feast of the Holy Innocents. *See* Childermas

"feasts of misrule", 115, 116–117, 158
final judgment, 32
fir, 211
Fire, 214
First Sunday in Advent, 27
    meditation, 28
    readings for, 27–28
Fischer, D. H., 96
forgiveness, 103
    power of thought, 103–104
    ritual of, 104–105
    as spiritual magic, 103–104
Fourth Sunday in Advent, 109
    Advent Wreath, 110
    lighting the fourth candle, 110–111
    meditation, 110
    reading for, 109–110
Saint Francis, 51, 84, 120
    Prayer of, 190–191
frankincense, 179, 180, 209–210
Friday, 83–84

Gaudete Sunday, 89
    Advent Wreath, 91
    lighting third candle, 91
    meditation, 90
    readings for, 89–90
genealogy, 143–144
Saint George, xxix
Glory be prayer, 188
Gnosticism, 114
    Sethian, 156
Gnostics, 114
gold, 179, 180
"Great Chain of Being", xxxiv
Greer, J. M., 121
Greeves, A., 33
Guardian Angel, 39–41
    prayer, 190
Gueranger, D., xxvii

Hades, 143
Hail, Holy Queen prayer, 189–190

Hail Mary prayer, 188
Heindel, M., 216
Henry II, King, 161, 163
history, 68
Holy Family, 165
    as family ideal, 165–167
    Justice, 166, 167–168
    meditation, 167–168
    practice, 167
"Holy Innocents", 157. *See* Childermas
Holy Name of Jesus, 170–171
Holy Spirit prayer, 188
holy water, making, 199–201
    exorcism of salt, 200
    exorcism of the water, 200–201
    ritual for holy water, 200
Howe, N., 35
Humanity's Karma, 78. *See also* Original Sin

iconography, 154
Immaculate Conception, 75, 145
    for Esoteric Christians, 78–79
    Original Sin, 75–78
    prayer and meditation, 79
impermanence. *See anicca*
incarnation, 146–147
Incarnation of Christ, 139
incense, 207
    natural incense, 209
    plants, 209–211
    resin incense, 208
    stick incense, 208–209
    types, 207–209
    use of, 207–209
infant Baptism, 76. *See also* Original Sin
"initiation", xiv–xv
intellect, xxvii, xxxi
intellectual, xxvii
Intellectual Plane, xxvii, 35. *See also* Law of the Planes
    angels, xxvii–xxviii
    eternity and, 35–36
    intellect in man, xxxi

Our Lady, xxx–xxxi
saints, xxviii–xxx

Janus, 169
Jesus Christ, 12, 104, 137, 166
    birth of, 146, 167
    Divine Mind, 141
    as history and myth, 33
    Holy Name of Jesus, 170–171
    Incarnation of Christ, 139
    return of. *See* Second Coming
    Sun and, 50
jia qi, 99
Saint Joachim, 76
Johannine group, 114
Saint John, 114, 154, 139
    etymology, 153
    Saint John's Day, 153
    meditation, 155–156
    ritual for blessing of wine, 154–155
    Solstice connection, 153
    and wine cup, 154
Saint John Chrysostom, 166
John Damascenus, 98
John the Baptist, 64–65, 90
Saint Joseph, 84, 146, 166, 167
Journey of Return, 141, 147
Judas, 96
juniper, 209
Jupiter, 213
Justice, 166, 167–168
Justina, 55, 56

kings and kingship, 163
Knight, G., 215

Law of Correspondence, xxxv
Law of the Planes, xxv
    angels, xxvii–xxviii
    Astral Plane, xxxi–xxxiii
    Energetic Plane, xxxiii–xxxiv
    intellect in man, xxxi
    Intellectual Plane, xxvii–xxxi
    material plane, xxxiv
    model of the planes, xxvi

Our Lady, xxx–xxxi
plane of unity or divine plane, xxvi–xxvii
saints, xxviii–xxx
Leadbeater, C. W., 210
Lewis, C. S., 33
Liberal Catholic Confiteor, 196
Limbo of the Infants (*Limbus Infantium*), 76
Lucifer, 143
Saint Lucy's Day, 93
    divination, 96
    "Little Yule", 94
    meditation, 95–96
    Saint Lucy, 93–94
    themes associated with, 95
    traditional celebrations, 94–95
Saint Luke, xxix, 146, 154

magical laws, xxv
    Law of Correspondence, xxxv
    Law of the Planes, xxv–xxxiv
magical philosophy, xxv
    devil and evil spirits, xxxiv
    Law of Correspondence, xxxv
    Law of the Planes, xxv–xxvi
    magical laws, xxv
The Magic of Catholicism (Brother A.D.A.), 215
magic, xv–xvi
    angel, 39
Magnificat prayer, 189
Saint Mark, 154
Mars, 213
Marsilio Ficino, xxvi
Mary. *See* Blessed Virgin Mary
material plane, xxxiv. *See also* Law of the Planes
Saint Matthew, 154
meditation, 15. *See also* prayer
Mercury, 214
Saint Michael the Archangel, xxxv, 84, 190
Miles, Clement A., 70, 115, 216
Moon, 214

mugwort, 210
myrrh, 179–180, 210
mysteries, list of, 197–198
myth, 32, 68
    Christ as history and, 33
    and Christian tradition, 32
    eschatology between event and, 36
    true myth, 33

New Year's Day, 169
    Feast of the Circumcision, 170–171
    Holy Name of Jesus, 170–171
    Janus, 169
    meditation, 171–172
    New Year's Resolution, 170
    traditional practices, 170
New Year's Eve, 169
    Party, 170
"next life", 37
The Nicene Creed, 193–194
Saint Nicholas Day, 67
    historical Saint Nicholas, 67–68
    legends of Saint Nicholas, 68–70
    meditation, 72–73
    Miles on, 70–71
    practices, 71–72
    traditions of, 70–71
novena, 46

Odysseus, 65
On the Divine Names (Dionysius the Areopagite), 120
orans posture, 17
Original Sin, 75–76. *See also* Immaculate Conception
    Collective Karma, 77–78
    consequences of, 76
    Eastern view, 76
    for Esoteric Christians, 77–78
    Humanity's Karma, 78
    infant Baptism, 76
    Past-Life Karma, 77
    Western view, 76
Orthodox Churches, 140
Our Father prayer, 187–188
Our Lady. *See* Blessed Virgin Mary
Our Lord. *See* Jesus Christ

Palo santo, 210
Paschasius, 94
Past-Life Karma, 77. *See also* Original Sin
patchouli, 210
Saint Patrick, xxix, 194–195
Saint Paul, 110, 166
Phaedo (Plato), 77
Physical Plane, 36
Pinchbeck, D., 162, 163
pine, 211
plane of unity, xxvi–xxvii. *See also* Law of the Planes
planetary and elemental correspondences, 213
    Air, 214
    Earth, 214
    Fire, 214
    Jupiter, 213
    Mars, 213
    Mercury, 214
    Moon, 214
    Saturn, 213
    Sun, 213
    Venus, 214
    Water, 214
Plato, 12, 65, 77, 162, 166
plausible deniability, 161
prayer, 15
    An Anglican prayer of Penitence, 195
    Canticle of the creatures (Song of the Sun), 191–193
    closing, 18
    common, 187
    The confession of faith of Saint Patrick, 194–195
    confiteor prayers, 195
    creeds and professions of faith, 193–195
    Fatima prayer, 190
    Glory be, 188
    Guardian Angel prayer, 190
    Hail, Holy Queen, 189–190
    Hail Mary, 188
    Holy Spirit prayer, 188
    Liberal Catholic Confiteor, 196

list of mysteries, 197–198
Magnificat, 189
Saint Michael prayer, 190
The Nicene Creed, 193–194
opening, 16–17
Our Father, 187–188
practice, 17
Prayer of Saint Francis, 190–191
The profession of faith of the Liberal Catholic Church, 195
Roman Catholic Confiteor, 195
The Rosary, 196–197
Proclus, 56
The profession of faith of the Liberal Catholic Church, 195
professions of faith. *See* creeds and professions of faith
Psalms, 9, 29, 203
Psalm, 5, 203–204
Psalm, 23, 204
Psalm, 46, 204–205
Psalm, 136, 205–206
psychic anatomy, 82, 162
Purgatory, xxix

qi nodes, 99
Queen of Heaven and Earth. *See* Blessed Virgin Mary
Queen of the Angels. *See* Blessed Virgin Mary

Rankin, D., 216
Saint Raphael the Archangel, 84
The Red Church (Bilardi), 215–216
repentance, 82
ritual
    banishing, 56–57
    for blessing of wine, 154–155
    for censing of house, 125–126
    Epiphany initiation, 180–182
    of forgiveness, 104–105
    for holy water, 200
    for protection, 56–57
Rituale Romanum, 123–124, 216
Roman Catholic Confiteor prayer, 195
The Rosary, 196–197
rose, 210

rosemary, 210
Rosicrucian Cosmo-Conception (Heindel), 216

sacramentals, 8, 123
    consecrating, 123–127
    ex opere operandis, 124
    ex opere operato, 124
    formula of blessing, 126–127
    holy water, 199
    power and practice of, 124
    Rituale Romanum, 123–124
    ritual for censing of house, 125–126
sage, 210–211
saints, xxviii–xxx
    Agatha, 94
    Andrew, xxix, 43–47
    Anna, 76
    Augustine, 76
    Blaise, xxix
    Dymphna, xxix
    Francis, 51, 84, 120, 190–191
    George, xxix
    Joachim, 76
    John, 114, 139, 153–155
    John Chrysostom, 166
    Joseph, 84, 146, 166, 167
    Lucy, 93–96
    Luke, xxix, 154
    Mark, 154
    Matthew, 154
    Nicholas, 67–73
    Patrick, xxix
    Paul, 110, 166
    Stephen, 149–152
    Therese of Lisieux, xxix, 84
    Thomas, 113–117
    Thomas Becket, 161–164
sandalwood, 211
Satan. *See* Lucifer
Saturn, 213
Second Coming, 31, 35–36
    Christ as history and myth, 33
    eschatology between myth and event, 36
    esoteric meaning of, 33–35

eternity and aeviternity, 32–33
eternity and Intellectual Plane, 35–36
final judgment, 32
meditation, 36–37
myth and Christian tradition, 32
true myth, 33
unpredictable apocalypse, 35
Second Sunday in Advent, 63
Advent Wreath, 65
meditation, 64–65
readings for, 63–64
Seraphim, xxvii, xxviii
Sethian Gnosticism, 156
Sign of the Cross, 55
as banishing ritual, 56–57
movements of divine power and banishing, 57–59
as protective magic, 55–56
ritual for protection, 56–57
sin, 143
"Solar Current", 59
Solomon, King, 104
soul, 82, 141
archetype of, 145
descent of, 142–143
redemption of, 146
spruce, 211
Saint Stephen's Day, 149
meditation, 151–152
Saint Stephen martyrdom, 149–150
traditional practices, 150–151
Strauss, W., 35
suffering. *See dukkha*
Summer Solstice, 153
Sun, 213
Sundays in Advent
first Sunday, 27–28
fourth Sunday, 109–111
second Sunday, 63–65
third Sunday. *See* Gaudete Sunday
symbolism, 154
Advent Wreath, 20–21
of candle, 29–30, 64, 90
Christmas Tree, 49–50
cross, 55
king, 163

talismans. *See* sacramentals
"Telluric Current", 59
Saint Therese of Lisieux, xxix, 84
third Sunday in Advent. *See* Gaudete Sunday
Saint Thomas, 113–114
customs, 116
"feasts of misrule", 115, 116–117
and Gnostic tradition, 114–115
Saint Thomas's Day, 113
Thomas's Gospel, 114
traditional celebrations, 115–116
Thomas à Becket. *See* Saint Thomas Becket
Saint Thomas Becket, 161
"Breaking Open the Head", 162–163
meditation, 164
practice, 163–164
Thomasites, 114
thought, power of, 103–104
Thrones, xxvii, xxviii
Tolkien, J. R. R., 33
traditions, xvi–xvii
true myth, 33
"true will", xvi

Uriel, archangel, 51

Venus, 214
"vibrate", 57
Voragine, J. de, 97, 100

Water, 214
Weiser, F. X., 216
William of Auxerre, 99
Winter of Solstice, 119
books of Holy Spirit, 119
celebrating, 120–121
world of Being, 34

"Yahweh", 153
yuan shen, 72

www.ingramcontent.com/pod-product-compliance
Ingram Content Group UK Ltd.
Pitfield, Milton Keynes, MK11 3LW, UK
UKHW021613220126
467229UK00012B/320